D1590056

The Silence
Of Surrendering Love
BODY, SOUL, SPIRIT INTEGRATION

The Silence of Surrendering Love

Body, Soul, Spirit Integration

By George A. Maloney, S.J.

ALBA · HOUSE   NEW · YORK

SOCIETY OF ST. PAUL, 2187 VICTORY BLVD., STATEN ISLAND, NEW YORK 10314

248.4
Mas

Library of Congress Cataloging in Publication Data

Maloney, George A., 1924-
   The silence of surrendering love.

   Bibliography: p.
   1. Silence — Religious aspects — Christianity.
I. Title.
BV4509.5.M257   1986   248.4'82   85-28636
ISBN 0-8189-0494-1

Imprimi Potest:
Vincent M. Cooke, S.J.
Provincial, New York Province

*Designed, printed and bound in the United States of
America by the Fathers and Brothers of the
Society of St. Paul, 2187 Victory Boulevard,
Staten Island, New York 10314, as part of their
communications apostolate.*

2 3 4 5 6 7 8 9 (Current Printing: first digit)

Dedication

To Mary Louise Leonard

Acknowledgments

GRATEFUL ACKNOWLEDGMENT is made to Darton, Longman & Todd, Ltd. and Doubleday & Company, Inc., N.Y. for excerpts from *The Jerusalem Bible*, copyright 1966 by Darton, Longman, Ltd. and Doubleday & Company, Inc. All scriptural texts are from this translation of the Bible, unless otherwise noted.

Great gratitude to Mrs. Rita Ruggiero for typing this manuscript and to Sister Joseph Agnes of the Sisters of Charity of Halifax for her proof-reading and many other suggestions in style.

Contents

Introduction

THERE HAVE BEEN many books and articles encouraging the busy modern man and woman to slow down and enter into an inner silence. Such authors give detailed descriptions of how we are to build up within ourselves an inner temple of silence. I do not wish to repeat what they have already written. I rather prefer to use the concept of silence as a model to describe the process of striving for human integration.

The great spiritual athletes of the 4th century who fled to the Egyptian deserts called such a process of becoming whole *divinization*. Silence on the body, soul and spiritual levels they called *hesychia*. Basically this word means *tranquility* and refers to the harmony of all human powers in an individual Christian under God's directing control. The risen Lord speaks His Word within us and the Holy Spirit gives us the ability, not only to recognize God's Word when spoken to us in this silence, but also the power to surrender to it and obey its commands.

Today much is being written by psychologists on how to expand our human consciousness. Religious writers, in turn, employ such findings to explain various ways of experiencing God. In this book, written for persons eager for deeper union with God and neighbor, I would like to describe the classical lines of the Christian spiritual life in terms of how to strive toward inner "attentiveness." On the one hand, this book is meant to encourage fellow-Christians to embrace all of the traditional disciplines of the ascetical life. In this respect it, hopefully, will inspire them to remove the obstacles and impediments that hold them back from a careful listening to God's Word within them and will help them, with God's grace, to obey that Word courageously. On the other hand, it is meant to encourage devout Christians to learn, through the silencing of all the negativity within their hearts, how to listen to God's unique Word, Jesus Christ, as He speaks within them each moment in the context of their concrete human situation.

Thus the concept of silence has two faces. One is concerned with the healing of all the forces from the outside world as well as from the inner psyche that habitually prevent our listening intensely and honestly to God's Word spoken in each moment. The other is to conceive silence as the loving milieu created within us through the healing and integration of all our powers in order that we may live in oneness of love with God and in loving oneness with each human person whom we are privileged on this earth to serve.

George A. Maloney, S.J.
Solemnity of the Mother of God, 1986

The Silence
Of Surrendering Love

CHAPTER ONE

Two Looks Devoured By Love

IN INGMAR BERGMAN'S movie, *Winter Light*, Pastor Tomas Eriksson seeks to give consolation, encouragement and counsel to one of his parishioners, a fear-tormented fisherman by the name of Jonas Persson. Persson is in anguish over his conviction that the Chinese are about to obtain the atom bomb with which they will bring about the eventual nuclear destruction of the world. And the Lutheran pastor, with all his pat words and high sounding phrases, is unable to touch the fisherman's heart and bring him peace. "If I speak with human tongues and angelic as well, but do not have love, I am a noisy gong, a clanging cymbal" (1 Cor 13:1). The main point of Bergman's movie is that if we are to be redeemed, it must be by the strong, persistent love of God who cloaks Himself in dreadful silence before our selfish, bombastic, pertinent (and impertinent) questionings.

On the eve of the third millennium, we stand before God and shout out with rage our demands that He speak to us as we wish that He would speak. But all we hear in reply is the echo of our own self-centered musings. We have effectively lost the ability to recognize the voice of God when He speaks His Word to us in silence and in love. We hear instead the insidious promptings of the demonic within us that — like a boa constrictor, wraps itself around our throats and suffocates us in a kind of living death. Such is the "silence" that most of us ever know. It is the "silence" created by the absence of speech and the lack of communication between man and God, God and man, and man and his fellow human being.

T.S. Eliot in his play, *The Cocktail Party*, has Celia, the Christ-figure of the play, describe as a cocktail party modern men and women and their inability to communicate with each other. "Everyone's alone — or so it seems to me. They make noises and think they are talking to each other. They make faces and think they understand each other. And I'm sure they don't."

The reason that we are unable to communicate with each other is that "we have not love," the love of God which is always permeated by the silence of God's Spirit. This silence, like love and life itself, cannot be bought or sold for a price and hence in the eyes of the world is totally "unprofitable," "useless." It should come as no surprise, therefore, that our *consumer*-oriented society ignores such silence as unreal or at least unworthy of its attention. Yet such silence — the silence which *divinizes* us and makes us whole — is the only thing that will ultimately prove profitable, useful and worthwhile. For "what does it profit a man if he gain the whole world but lose himself in the process?" It is in this silence that we come in touch with the Source of all reality, God Himself.

Sören Kierkegaard, the great Danish philosopher, wrote about such genuine silence and the urgency on our part to attain it when he stated:

> *The present state of the world and the whole of life is diseased. If I were a doctor and were asked for my advice, I should reply: Create Silence! Bring men to silence. The Word of God cannot be heard in*

the noisy world of today. And even if it were blazoned forth with all the panoply of noise so that it could be heard in the midst of all the other noise, then it would no longer be the Word of God. Therefore, create silence.

The Silence Of God

ST. PAUL tells us to "speak the truth with love" (Ep 4:15). But our words must be surrounded by silence, God's silence, if they are to ring true. In God we see that silence is not opposed to words, but true Word-communication comes from the silence of the Spirit and continues to be spoken and lived out in the same silence of the Spirit. Perhaps a very good way to understand God's silence is to study the classic Byzantine icon of the Trinity painted by the Russian monk, Andrei Rublev (c. 1408-1425). This painting is a mystical vision, through harmony and relationship of colors and circular lines, of the inner trinitarian life of movement and rest, peace and joy, of a community of three in one. The Godhead is a nameless form which constantly feeds back through its circular movement from one person to the other two.

In this icon we see three angels, the heavenly visitors to Abraham at the oak of Mambre (Gn 18), depicting the three Persons in the Trinity. The Father is shown as the angel on the left, as a figure subdued and retiring, suggesting the apophatic belief in the unknowability directly of the Father or the Godhead of the Trinity except through the Son who is the angelic figure in the center. He dominates the entire icon as He gazes lovingly at the Father while pointing His two fingers, symbolical of His two natures, divine and human, toward the eucharistic chalice on the white table before them. The Holy Spirit is seen as the third angel on the right dressed in a green cloak, the sign of youth and fullness of powers.

Before there are Divine Persons, in inter-communion with each other in expressed love, there is the Godhead. This Godhead is the Abyss of Silence. It is not non-being out of which comes the being of the three persons. It is God as "unnatured nature," to use Meister Eckhart's phrase. It is non-being for it contains all beings. It is *nowhere* for it cannot be contained in its wildness before it becomes tamed by love. It is the ocean before fish have been created. It is the air before birds have been made to fly. It is the fullness of the Uncreated before the spark ignites and hurls intelligence toward loving union. It is where total poverty meets infinite richness. It is Infinite Zero from which everyone and everything radiates and to which all lovingly return.

The Richness Of The Godhead

BECAUSE of the Godhead's infinite richness, it cannot be classified in quantified numbers or in categories of beings that have an origin of their being. The Godhead is beyond all being and yet is found in all being, including the Trinity and ourselves. Nietzsche once wrote: "One must possess a chaos within to give birth to a star." It is here that the Father becomes the Father of His Son through the silent love of the Holy Spirit who proceeds from both the Father and the Son. Two looks devoured by Love! It is here that we are led in silent adoration and contemplation to a knowing beyond our knowing. In silence we come into the Void. We merge with the darkness of the Godhead. No longer is God an "object" toward which we go in prayer to communicate in order to receive some "things." The ocean covers everything and does not need to become wet since all things are wet because of its complete covering of everything.

Like the crackling sound of a fiery spark that shoots
through the rain-soaked heavens, a movement stirs within
non-movement; a light moves through darkness. Out of the
Void God stirs as personal Source, the Father who wishes
from all eternity to share His fullness of being. The Mind
wishes to think a thought, a word, in order to know Himself
as the Begetter of the Word.

The Father moves the Godhead from pure repose and
absolute silence to meaningful, loving motion as He pours
the fullness of His divinity into His Son (Col 2:9). What we
could never know, God's Word has revealed to us. God is a
community, a family of loving persons.

It is an ecstatic, loving intimacy of a Father emptying
Himself into His Son through His Spirit of love. Such intimacy and self-emptying are returned by the Son's gifting
Himself back to the Father through the same Spirit. Jesus
reveals that in the Trinity is the secret of life which unfolds
in silence, the language of love. Love is a call to receive one's
being in the intimate self-surrendering of the other. In the
ecstasy of "standing outside" of oneself and becoming available through the gift of love to live for the other, Father and
Son and Holy Spirit, all come into their unique *being* as
distinct yet united persons. The *I* is the child of the *We*. God
as Trinity is the revelation that uniqueness of persons comes
only from a family of two or more persons in love. In the
very self-giving of the Father to the Son and the Son to the
Father a third Person has His *being*. The Holy Spirit proceeds, not as another Word, but from the silent love of the
Father for the Son and the silent single Word, the Son,
surrendering to the Father. The Spirit is silent Love, experienced but not heard except in the soundlessness of Love
itself.

Silence And The Trinity

THE AWESOME MYSTERY of the Trinity, which is the beginning and end of all reality, reveals to us a transcendent truth that should permeate the whole of our lives. Out of Absolute Silence the Godhead could not yet experience community. For an I-Thou relationship, bringing forth a *We*-community, could come only when the Father spoke in relative silence His Word. That relative silence we call the Holy Spirit.

It is the cosmic bird that hovers over the chaos and the void. It stirs the *I* of the Heavenly Father to perceive Himself as one not isolated. The Spirit which is the Spirit of Love, moves the heart of the Father, and the Son is begotten in the silent Word that the Father utters. The Father thrills to see Himself imaged, as Mind discovers itself in the Word that issues from the Mind. But He thrills also to discover Himself as the unique Father of His Son when the Son in the power of the silent Spirit utters His silent *Yes* in total self-surrender to the Father.

We — patterned on God's image and likeness (Gn 1:26) — project that image most often not in the negative silence of chosen isolation and mutism but in speech. But the words we speak must proceed from the same silent Spirit of love and return "home" to that Spirit. We move away from imaging God as He speaks His Word in the silent love of the Spirit when we fail to speak our words in God's love.

It is through God's Spirit of Love that He has the name Father. His fatherhood is expressed in His silent, eternal self-giving to His Son. St. Hilary of Poitiers insists that the Father and the Son have a perfect, mutual knowledge, which exists because of their mutual relationship of Father and Son to each other. If the Father and Son mutually know themselves, this is brought about necessarily by the Holy

Spirit who allows them in silence, not only mutually to affirm themselves as Father and Son, but mutually to recognize themselves as such.

The Father and Son know themselves in that primal act of "emptying," the abyss of deepest silence as a primal attribute of love, of the Father into the Son and the Son's "emptying" of Himself into the Father in mutual self-surrender. This is nothing but the binding force of the Holy Spirit as Love. The Holy Spirit cannot be an accidental relation, a "thing" produced, but in a mysterious manner it is the Holy Spirit who unites the Father and Son eternally in love which cannot be separated from the knowing by the Father in His Son. The Spirit unites and yet "proceeds" both from the Father and the Son and has His whole being in the unifying "gasp" of silent love that individualizes the Father and the Son. Such Love proceeding is Love in its primal silence. The Spirit cannot be another Word spoken by the Mind for that would break the eternal silence. The Spirit is the "kenotic" or emptying Love that cannot be objectivized nor heard as a Word but can only be experienced in the presence of two becoming one.

From this three-fold movement, therefore, all reality within the Trinity and without flows, i.e. in the order of creation and God's shared being through His uncreated energies of love. For the Father to know Himself in His expressed Word is not enough. Such knowledge must be completed by love since it is through love that one "knows" most truly. Knowledge is experienced from the very first movement of self-giving. Love completes knowledge and, although knowledge and love are not the same, within the Trinity both the Son's identity *as known* in the love of the Father and *as knowing* the Father in His returned love is rendered possible only through *realized love* which is the Spirit proceeding from both the Father and the Son. Known and knowing both proceed from the one Source, the Spirit, though differently.

Explosion Love

OUR WEAK MINDS cannot fathom the peace and joy, the ardent excitement and exuberant self-surrender that flow in perfect silence in a reposeful movement between Father and Son through the Holy Spirit. God becomes real only because He can communicate in Love with His Word. His Word gives Him identity as Father. But that means eternal self-giving to the Other, His Word in Love, the Holy Spirit.

Such an "implosion" of love between Father and Son through the Spirit seemingly is not enough. Such tremendous Love within the Trinity, we learn only from Scripture, seeks to "explode" outside of its own community. God in His humility wishes to create new life that can share in His ecstatic love within the Trinity. We human beings know this to be our experience of an *I-Thou* love relationship that stretches outward to share that love in new love and in the creation of new life. And this is true because it is first true of God, the Source of all participated life and love.

Richard of St. Victor (+1173) explains why the Trinity seeks to share itself in self-giving. True love seeks to be totally self-sacrificing on behalf of the one loved. But such a love wants to be shared with another. Thus an *I* and *Thou* move into a *We*-community of three persons, equally loving each other with the very same love. He writes:

> *When one gives love to another and when he alone loves the other alone, there is love certainly but not shared love. When two love each other and give each other their most ardent affection and when the affection of the first flows to the second and that of the second to the first, moving as it were in different directions, there is love on*

both sides certainly, but there is not shared love. Strictly speaking, there is shared love when two persons love a third in a harmony of affection and a community of love and when the loves of the two converge in the single flame of love they have for the third . . . From this, then, it is evident that shared love would not have a place in the divinity if there were only two persons and not a third.

It is only faith received through God's revelation found in the Old and New Testaments that opens us to accept the Good News that the trinitarian community of Father and Son and Holy Spirit moves outward to create a world of participated beauty. Among all His material creatures, there stands one, the human person, who is gifted to be able to communicate with the Trinity. Man is given a share in God's very own divine nature (2 P 1:4). We are called in God's humility to receive His emptying love as self-gift of Father, Son and Holy Spirit. Our calling is to enter into God's primal silence and hear His Word of Love, Jesus Christ, tell us at each moment of our earthly journey how great is His love. We are called to answer in the shared silence of the Word as we, with Him, repeat our constant "Yes" in total silence.

St. Paul gives us a summary in non-speculative terms of the movement of the divine We-community into our world in order to share with us human beings the same relationships enjoyed between Father and Son as *I-Thou*, brought together in perfect, silent, loving union by the Spirit. The Spirit fashions a *We*-community that in God's holiness and humility stretches down to engulf us also into that intimate, trinitarian community through the Body of Christ in His Spirit:

Blessed be God the Father of our Lord Jesus Christ, who has blessed us with all the spiritual blessings of heaven in Christ.

Before the world was made, he chose us, chose us in Christ,
to be holy and spotless, and to live through love in his presence,
determining that we should become his adopted sons, through
        Jesus Christ
. . . to make us praise the glory of his grace,
his free gift to us in the Beloved . . .
He has let us know the mystery of his purpose,
the hidden plan he so kindly made in Christ from the beginning. . .
that he would bring everything together under Christ, as head,
everything in the heavens and everything in earth.
. . . Now you too, in him,
have heard the message of the truth and the good news of your
        salvation,
and have believed it;
and you too have been stamped with the seal of the Holy Spirit of
        the Promise,
the pledge of our inheritance
which brings freedom for those whom God has taken for his own,
to make his glory praised (Ep 1:3-14).

CHAPTER TWO

God's Silence In Creation

FROM WITHIN the flaming heart of the Trinity, God's explosive love has burst forth in a personalized sharing of that love with creatures. At the heart of the Trinity, as in the eye of a hurricane, there is only silence and repose. Yet from such a "still-point" God uttered His Word in the atmosphere of the silent love of the Spirit and matter was created. St. John tells us that through God's Word — the Word which was with Him in the beginning — all things were made. "Through Him all things came to be, not one thing had its being but through Him" (Jn 1:3). The Psalmist grasped the creative power of God's Word when he affirmed that

> *By the word of Yahweh the heavens were made,*
> *their whole array by the breath of His mouth,*
> *He collects the ocean waters as though in a wineskin,*
> *He stores the deeps in cellars (Ps 33:6).*

Of its very nature, love is prolific. If God's essence is love, then it must necessarily follow that He seeks by nature to share His very being. Our Judeo-Christian tradition teaches us that God becomes a God-toward-others by communicating Himself through His Word and His Spirit, Love. St. Irenaeus in the 2nd century describes God the Father as reaching out in the act of creation to fashion the entire world with His own two hands: The Word Made Flesh (Jesus Christ) and the Holy Spirit.

God creates the whole world as good, as a sign of His burning desire to give Himself in faithful communication through His Word. The world at its center is filled with the self-communicating Trinity. God is filling the universe with His loving Self. His uncreated energies whirl through space and fill all creatures with His loving, creative presence. "He spoke, and it was created; he commanded and there it stood" (Ps 33:9).

There Is Only The Dance

A WHOLE WORLD of beautiful creatures: seas and rivers, mountains and plains, birds and fish, animals and men, stars and moon, sun and planets tumble from the finger tips of God, the Supreme Artist. Through the electron microscope we can peer into a world that was previously only hinted at by a handful of God's chosen prophets and mystics. We find nothing in the universe to be static. All creatures — molecules, atoms, electrons, protons, neutrons and even quarks — move and vibrate in a cosmic symphony of harmony and grace. T.S. Eliot beautifully describes God's eternal life as the source of all created life, as a *dance* at the still point of the turning world:

> At the still point of the turning world. Neither flesh
>   nor fleshless;
> Neither from nor towards; at the still point, there the dance is,
> But neither arrest nor movement. And do not call it fixity.
> Where past and future are gathered. Neither movement from nor
>   towards,
> Neither ascent nor decline. Except for the point, the still point,

There would be no dance, and there is only the dance.
I can only say, there we have been; but I cannot say where.
And I cannot say how long, for that is to place it in time.

(Burnt Norton)

Quantum physicists speak no longer of created matter as a solid mass. They speak more and more in the language of mystics. Everything in the cosmos is inter-connected and moves in a harmonious wholeness. Each part has its proper place within the universe. Each creature depends on and gives support to all the others in one great body, all of which in the belief of Christianity is being created in and through God's Word with the cooperation of human beings. How beautifully this is brought out in Psalm 104:

> *Yahweh, what variety you have created,*
> *arranging everything so wisely!*
> *Earth is completely full of things you have made:*
> *among them the vast expanse of ocean.*
> *teeming with countless creatures,*
> *creatures large and small . . .*
> *You give breath, fresh life begins,*
> *you keep renewing the world (Ps 104:24-25, 30).*

You and I have been living in God's rhythm and harmony of love from the very first moment of our conception. We pulsate — along with every molecule and atom throughout this one gigantic, evolving universe — in an inner silence that is filled with God's uncreated energies of directing love. George Leonard, former senior editor of *Look* magazine, writes of this exciting world in evolution:

> *At the heart of each of us, whatever our imperfections, there exists a*
> *silent pulse of perfect rhythm, a complex of wave forms and reso-*
> *nances, which is absolutely individual and unique, and yet which*

connects us to everything in the universe. The act of getting in touch with this pulse can transform our personal experience and in some way alter the world around us (The Silent Pulse; *Preface xii*).

From Chaos To Chaos

BUT WE human beings, made a little less than God (Ps 8:5), used our very gifts of intellect and will to pull out of this rhythmic dance. By sin we introduced our own noisy self-centeredness into our world as we slipped away from the inner, silent Spirit of God's care inviting us to hear His Word and lovingly to obey Him. We have wandered far from God's intended evolutive plan and from that time when man and woman — as Genesis describes it — lived in harmony with one another, with God and with all of nature. The material world was meant to be the setting in which man and woman would express their love by means of their own creative work in fashioning the world according to God's Word. But our spiritual eyes were blinded by our sin, and we no longer see God everywhere. A rose to most of us is merely a rose and nothing more. Seeing the world that our anthropocentric view of the universe has created, we ask ourselves: what is it that is blinding us to God's inner presence in whom all things really do live and move and have their being (Ac 17:28)? Is it possible to return to the still point of the turning world — to God, where there is only harmony in His silent love? Or must we sit, each of us alone, shaking with nameless fears and anxieties that riddle our bodies, souls and spirits?

Modern technology has created its own Frankenstein. It has produced its own demonic force that is blanketing the earth with a destructive power that is propelling the world toward a universal cataclysm at an alarming rate each day.

Water and air pollution, the pillage of mineral resources, the increasing list of extinct or endangered birds and animals, the far-reaching effects of pesticides, the wanton dumping of industrial chemicals on land and sea, the overwhelming accumulation of waste, garbage and junk, the spiraling of the population explosion, the very real possibility of a nuclear holocaust and the millions of aborted fetuses each year, all add up to a scenario of apocalyptic proportions.

Yet all of these are but outward signs of a still more terrible, interior threat that is gnawing away at our mental and spiritual powers. Destructive thoughts and impulses, uncontrolled desires and feelings, free-floating fears and anxieties are crippling our ability to live lives of joy and meaningfulness. What ever happened to romance and idealism, to noble man and woman who once danced joyously to soft music, thrilled to climb snow-capped mountains, loved to break bread with friends and enjoy a cup of wine?

God Speaks Silently Through His Word

YET GOD is still within His creatures. He has never ceased speaking to us through the creative force that is His Word, "for in Him were created all things in heaven and on earth" (Col 1:16). Creation in a very real sense is God's speech materialized. All created things speak to us of God. God's silence, an infinite potentiality of rich, shared knowledge and love, would have exploded had it not expressed itself in such an "utterance." But God did and does share His *being* with His creatures through His creative Word. In the Old Testament, and surely also in the mind of the writer of the Johannine corpus, *Word* (*Dabar*, in Hebrew) is a dynamic concept, totally dependent on God who communicates His mind through His Word to us. In each creature God speaks His Word and creates in that creature a participated word, a principle of harmony which reveals to us, if we but listen attentively to that word in creation, its relationship to God's total order of salvation. The whole created world is interlocked and interrelated, but only we human beings, of all God's material creatures, are capable of appreciating the harmonious relationship to any given created *logos* and God's spoken Word, the *Logos*.

Another part of the Hebraic understanding of *Dabar* has to do not only with the intellectual concept of what makes up the *thisness* of each created nature but also with the dynamic power which God's Word releases in the "listener" to the logos in this or that creature. The *Word* is charged with creative power and energy which flow from the Divine Word into the receiver, transforming him somewhat into the Word and the Mind speaking the Word.

Only human persons have been given the power to discover the *Logos* and the *logoi* in all creation and to work lovingly to bring all things into harmony through and in and for the Logos (Col 1:20). Only man is open-ended and able to respond to God's desire that he cooperate in the completion, not only of his own creation of himself into the person God sees him to be in His Word, but to bring about the fulfillment of other creatures by working in loving service with and on behalf of the Word made flesh, the risen Lord Jesus Christ.

Our Uniqueness As Human Beings

OUR UNIQUENESS over all other creatures consists in our having been made by God to be self-positing creatures. The image of God in us consists ultimately in possessing the spiritual faculties of intellect and will through which instruments we may posit ourselves as individual *Is*, dependent on the Absolute *I* of God. Genesis, as the early Fathers interpreted its story of our creation by God, indicates by the use of "image and likeness" that our total being has its meaning in the Prime Image of God, namely the Logos, the Divine Word that mirrors forth, as the Speech of God, the incomprehensible Mind of God.

God created us, not as totally independent beings, but precisely as self-positing beings in reference to a Prototype. That Prototype is the Divine Word, the "Image of the invisible God," as St. Paul describes Christ (Col 1:15) and according to whose image and likeness we have all been created. We are not, therefore, images of the Father but in our very being we mirror a very special relationship to Him in and through Jesus. He is the perfect Image. We are made according to that Image. Emil Brunner beautifully describes this ontological relationship to God through the Word when he writes:

> *God creates man in such a way that in this very creation man is summoned to receive the Word actively, that is, he is called to listen, to understand, and to believe. God creates man's being in such a way that man knows that he is determined and conditioned by God, and in the Divine "Thou," or, more exactly, from and in the Divine Word, whose claim 'calls' man's being into existence. . . The characteristic imprint of man, however, only develops on the basis of Divine determination, as an answer to a call, by means of a decision. The necessity for a decision, an obligation which he can never evade, is the distinguishing feature of man. . .(It) is the being created by God to stand 'over-against' Him, who can reply to God, and who in this answer alone fulfills — or destroys — the purpose of God's creation.* (Man in Revolt)

But we are to listen and obey the Word, Jesus Christ, who lives in us through His resurrectional presence. He communicates directly and immediately to us to the degree that we have silenced our own voices and selfish clamorings. But He also communicates in silence His living presence in the evolutive process of bringing all other creatures which surround us into their own uniqueness. The total creation will ultimately be the total Christ (Col 3:11). This is what St. Ignatius of Antioch (+105) meant when he wrote in his epistle to the Ephesians: "Anyone who is really possessed of the word of Jesus can listen to His silence and so be perfect; so that he may act through his words and be known by his silence."

Our Need For Silence

ONE OF THE greatest needs we have in our modern world is the need to be silent in order to hear God speak His Word at all times. Our lives, though, move at such neck-breaking speeds. Where will we find the time? So many things demand our attention. Unless we are rooted in the silence of God's Word and His harmony, we risk being filled with all kinds of anxieties and fears about the ultimate meaninglessness of it all. If we lack an attitude of *at-oneness* with the things that bombard us as objects to be conquered or fled from, our immersion in the pragmatic materialism which surrounds us will soon suffocate our communion with God's Spirit of silent love. Thus, cut off from an experienced relationship with God — the Absolutely Transcendent and yet intimately indwelling Trinity — we are adrift on a dark and dangerous sea that threatens our very purpose in life. The Austrian psychiatrist, Viktor E. Frankl, explains our plight in the modern world in these words: "Effectively an ever-increasing number of our clients today suffer from a feeling of interior emptiness — which I have described as existential emptiness — a feeling of total absence of a meaning to existence."

How recently have you had the impulse to leave your busy world and get away from it all by going out to the "country," to some quiet place close to the rhythm of nature and of God's inner silent presence? How we need to break away from our fragmented world that is so constantly filled with noises, disharmony and apparent meaninglessness! We need from time to time to enter into God's primal time, the *now* of God's unchangeable silent love for us, and there to become regenerated. In such places, life and love merge into the same experience.

To be alone with the Alone in silence and solitude is a virtual necessity for our physical, mental and spiritual wholeness. It is only in returning to such moments of stillness and quiet that we ever make genuine progress in our spiritual growth. It is only in silence that we are able to listen well to God's Word as He speaks to us of His eternal love for us. ". . . in quietness and in confidence shall be your strength" (Is 30:15).

The Physical Silence Of Nature

ALTHOUGH MOST of us cannot regularly live in primeval natural surroundings, nevertheless, we do need to find occasions when we can enter into the stillness of a woods near an isolated mountain stream, or take a solitary walk along a deserted ocean beach somewhere, or meditate beneath the over-hanging boughs of nature's own cathedrals which draw our hearts upward toward God. Once I had an opportunity to spend three months on a farm, quite alone, in Georgia. In the evening, especially, it was incredibly refreshing and regenerating to sit by the lake and watch the sun go down upon the quiet waters. As night brought peace and rest to all of nature, frogs and unseen insects began their nightly chorus. At dawn your spirit could not help but rise along with the flaming colors that spangled the scattered clouds of morn. The birds would sing the world awake with notes of hopeful joy. Did not Jesus Himself invite us to "come apart and rest awhile" (Mk 6:31)? We all of us need discipline if we are to enter into God's quiet and drink in the beauty of His nature. Especially do we need it if we are to discover the inner beauty already buried deep within our hearts.

No doubt it was in such a moment of solitude with God that St. Augustine wrote: "Heaven and earth and all that is in the universe cry out to me from all directions that I, O God, must love Thee, and they do not cease to cry out to all so that they have no excuse." In such moments we are lifted outside of our habitual selves and we seem to be able to stretch out and touch God in the beauties of nature. We are filled with reverence as we contemplate the wonder of it all and we feel a new oneness with the Absolute. All barriers seem to crumble and we merge easily into God's loving presence. We *are!* There is need for no words, no activity; just surrender in silence. Such a peak experience drew out of the enflamed heart of Blaise Pascal the cry: "The eternal silence of those boundless spaces strikes awe into my soul."

Siddhartha in Hermann Hesse's novel learned the secret of life by listening to the ancient but ever new river speak to him. Yet God is silently dancing His presence into our lives in the context of our daily environment. One of the great dangers of modern life is that we have been allowing our senses to atrophy through our thermostated, computer controlled existences. We find it difficult to hear the music in a child's voice, the rhythm of the traffic, the steady beat of our own heart. The touch of cool, cleansing water on a sweaty face has lost its restorative meaning for us. The taste of warm, freshly baked bread on hungry lips, the smell of the ozone in the air after a clearing rain, are lost experiences for most of us. And so we live only in noise and disharmony and fail to enter into God's silence and harmony all around us. Thus we close ourselves off from the possibility of God's communicating to us through His material world.

Listening To God With Our Senses

WE HAVE a great need today to re-educate our senses in order that they bring to our consciousness sharp, vital, fully felt experiences, the only way in which the material world can make contact with our interior selves. We discover the silent, loving God living within us by listening to Him with our senses which are in touch with God's presence in His wonderful, material creation.

Abstract and pop art can help awaken our eyes to "see" deeply in color and dimension. If alert, we can also learn how to make contact with God immanently present in all His created, material world as we walk the concrete pavements of our big cities. We can learn to see the beauty of the cross and the promise of resurrection in a tiny drop of water lying in a dirty, urban street. In that drop of water we can train ourselves to see the different colors of God's world — a world in which He is vitally immersed and dynamically working — reflected as in a mirror. The symbol of a drop of water in a Harlem gutter, able to mirror the whole world around it, can lead us to reflect upon the promise and the hope of a newly cleansed life in God.

We have no other way to meet God but by beginning with His created world. In the commonplace activities of our life, in the sense experiences overly familiar to us from a lifetime of routine, in every human being whom we encounter physically, we have a contact point with God. "Kneel down, this place is holy!" God proclaims His loving presence all around us, but only those who are silent in their heart can hear Him speak His word of love.

Fear Of Being Alone

GOD WANTS us to discover ourselves in the exchange of love that comes through our communion with other human beings and with God. And it is partly for that reason that we find it hard to be alone. We mistake being alone with loneliness. And we fear loneliness for at least two reasons. One is that the isolation which we feel when we are lonely opens up a lot of smouldering, hellish experiences that lie deep within our consciousness. We are forced to confront the brokenness, the guilt and the fears which cripple us and hold us in bondage to a very low self-esteem. We tend to see such loneliness as a rejection of ourselves on the part of others. This, in turn, builds up more fear and even stronger convictions that we are worthless and that no one truly loves us.

How we shrink from the discipline of quieting our bodies, minds and spirits when it entails being alone! We will do just about anything to distract ourselves from such a call to be still and know that God is our God (Ps 46:10). Without such quiet, yes, even confronting the darkness within us, there can be no growth in deeper, prayerful union with the Lord. Attentive listening to the Word of God which can be heard only by silencing the noises in our hearts, is a dying process to that autonomous "managerial" hold we have over our lives. Above all, we must let go of the hold we think we have on God as we busily fashion images of Him that become static little idols before which we bow and do reverence.

But the living God of Abraham, Isaac and Jacob waits for

us in the desert of our silent selves to reveal Himself to us in His own time and in His own words. If we develop the habit of stopping often during the day to come to our center where God dwells — who is also the Center of the boundless universe — we will soon discover that God truly speaks His Divine Word from deep down within us. We all find time to read the newspapers, to watch TV, especially for the daily news, to eat our daily meals, to socialize with our loved ones and friends, to work and work hard. We ought also to give some time in the early morning and before going to bed to enter into that "seventh day of rest" where we are swept up into the powerful Center of our lives and of all reality.

Scripture says: "After all his work, God rested on the seventh day" (Gn 2:2; Heb 4:4). We, too, need to learn to rest in His loving, silent presence. He does communicate to us through His Word. As He so softly speaks His creative Word throughout all of nature, so too He speaks His Word when we silence our busy bodies, souls and spirits and become one with all things in the quieting harmony that moves in rhythmic dance through all of God's creation. Happy will those be who can go to the Center who lives at the heart of all created matter to find Him who has no boundaries and yet is in all things.

Riding along the highway to work and "feeling" the rhythm of the car on the road can put us into synch with God and all of nature. Listening to raindrops falling gently on the roof as we seek sleep can be a great quieting force. Looking at a flower, a lighted candle in a darkened room, a crucifix, a picture of some scenic wonder, or even focusing our attention on the powerful, quieting harmony in uplifting music — all of these can help us to reach that "still point" where God is met most powerfully and where He most clearly speaks to us His saving, healing Word. Christianity is a holistic religion which, by God's power and our human cooperation, unifies our powers of body, soul and spirit. As we become quieted in all our members, we can reach the oneness of all things in Christ.

Prayer Exercise

OUR HUMAN existence on this earth is literally a walk, a journey. We are continually moving from one place to another, from home to work, from relatives or friends back to home, from home to church, to the store, to the movies. How much more on a spiritual plane do our lives unfold on different levels of awareness of our oneness with God and with the world around us. When we quiet our persons enough to listen to God's silent presence in and about us, we are ready for prayer. Prayer is ultimately listening in love to God and surrendering to Him in the fullness of our being in worship and adoration.

On your next walk, choose a place that is peaceful, where God can be sensed permeating the beauties of nature. Stand silently for a moment. Feel God's energies silently move through your entire body from head to toe. Relax and allow your arms to hang loosely at your side. Begin to walk. Breathe in deeply with your very first strides. Keep in step with your breathing. Strike a walking rhythm that fits you. Give it a pattern, for example, of four steps as you slowly breathe in and five or six as you breathe out. Seek to lengthen your exhalation and, therefore, take more steps as you breathe out than as you breathe in.

Feel the physical harmony and rhythm in all parts of your body. Enter wholly into the walk with a sense of joy and new life. Be aware of the contact your feet make with the ground. Listen to the noise. Feel the impact. Unite your breathing in and out and the movement of your body to your psyche and spirit. Become consciously one with God, Father, Son and Spirit living within you.

Peacefully observe the world around you. Lose yourself in the long silence of God who has been so patiently creating this or that tree over so many years. Enjoy the quiet movement of a butterfly that passes by, the bird or the bug on the road. All silently proclaim to you that in Him they live and move and have their being (Ac 17:28). Smell the fragrances in the air from flowers, trees and grass. Let your heart silently express the love it feels towards God and all His creatures, including yourself. Recognize your own beauty. Appreciate your dignity as a child of God and a privileged part of His creation — a being who is one with God and nature. Surrender to Him in silent love.

Learn to walk this way at home, at work, in church or wherever you are. Consciously seek to be one with the Trinity Who is within you and Who leads you from noise to silence, from darkness into greater light, from a lower level of human existence to an ever-increasing, dynamic living totally for God in adoration.

CHAPTER THREE

A Still Silent Voice

METEOROLOGISTS have studied hurricanes and have discovered that at the eye of their violent, swirling, destructive winds there is a center of calm and peace. Motion and violence outside; but within the inner eye there is motionless tranquillity.

The prophet Elijah is a model for all of us as he went up Mount Horeb to discover God in the solitude of a hidden cave. God, we read, spoke to him not in the "hurricane" that sundered the mountain and shattered its rocks. Nor did He communicate His Word in the violent earthquake or in the blazing fire. God rather spoke His Word to him in the tiny whispering sound of a gentle breeze.

> *Then Yahweh himself went by. There came a mighty wind, so strong it tore the mountains and shattered the rocks before Yahweh. But Yahweh was not in the earthquake. After the earthquake came a fire. But Yahweh was not in the fire. And after the fire there came the sound of a gentle breeze. And when Elijah heard this, he covered his face with his cloak and went out and stood at the entrance of the cave (1 K 19:12-13).*

If we are to be in communication with God through His Word, we, too, need to "in-merge" ourselves deep within the

hidden cave of our hearts and there listen to God speak to us
in the silence "of a gentle breeze." Then, and only then, can
we "e-merge" as doers sent and empowered by God to
enflesh — by loving service to others — the Word that we
have heard from God in us. But have we become true
listeners by silencing the noises from within? Are we not so
off-center at times that it is we ourselves rather than God
that we listen to? And when we think that we are honestly
ready and willing to listen to God speak His Word, do we not
wait for the words we wish to hear?

Thomas Merton describes the paradox of *emptying* silence as a true filling up with the richness of God Himself, as
something that is a higher kind of listening and not a receptivity to a certain kind of message. It is a general emptying "that waits to realize the fullness of the message of God
within its own apparent void. The true contemplative . . .
remains empty because he knows that he can never expect
or anticipate the word that will transform his darkness into
light" (*Contemplative Prayer*, p. 112).

Before The Burning Bush

MOSES before the burning bush teaches us how we are to let
go of our own desire to control God. He was in the desert
tending his father-in-law Jethro's flocks when he saw a bush
aflame yet unconsumed. Being curious, he approached to
examine with his own critical powers this strange phenomenon. As Moses advanced to see why the bush was not burning, Yahweh called to him from the middle of the bush:
"Moses, Moses! . . . Come no nearer. Take off your shoes, for
the place on which you stand is holy ground. I am the God of
your fathers, the God of Abraham, the God of Isaac and the
God of Jacob" (Ex 3:3-4). Then Moses covered his face,
afraid to look at the awesome, transcendent God.

To approach God, the fullness of all being, the Center that has no circumference, there is need on our part to leave something behind, as a caterpillar must leave one lower level to become a chrysalis, only to leave that stage to emerge as a beautiful butterfly.

It is God who calls us by inviting us to inner silence: "Be still and know I am your God" (Ps 46:10, KJV). He chooses us, as He did Moses, to do a special work. But to hear His Word we must leave behind our noisy self-centeredness and enter into a greater surrendering intimacy with Him. The Divine Bridegroom invites us, His Brides, to enter into a deeper life with Him:

> *Come then, my love,*
> *my lovely one, come.*
> *For see, winter is past,*
> *the rains are over and gone.*
> *The flowers appear on the earth.*
> *The season of glad songs has come,*
> *the cooing of the turtledove is heard in our land (Sg 2:10-12).*

To enter into this deeper intimacy with God and to surrender completely to His ways we are in need of that inner silence that stops our own flow of ideas about God and His plans. In true surrendering love, we can then listen and hear God's still, soft voice.

A God we can control is not the one God, living and true, the God of Abraham, Isaac and Jacob, but one we have invented to satisfy our own needs. Nietzsche once wrote, "A thing explained ceases to interest us; this is why God will always interest us." We are called by God to meet Him in faith and not in the relatively clear vision of our intellect. "Now we are seeing a dim reflection in a mirror; but then we shall be seeing face to face. The knowledge that I have now is imperfect; but then I shall know as fully as I am known" (1 Cor 13:12).

Moses teaches us not to advance, not to try to seize God by our own powers — intellectual or otherwise — but rather to fall back before the burning bush in humility and adoration. Our bare feet are a symbol of the fact that we have shed all our pretensions in this regard. God is a consuming fire (Heb 12:29). His love "is a flash of fire, a flame of Yahweh himself" (Sg 8:6).

Nikos Kazantzakis describes the surrender we must make to God the great Fire: "God is fire and you must walk on it . . . dance on it. At that moment the fire will become cool water. But until you reach that point, what a struggle, my Lord, what agony!" God as fire illumines and transforms us to the degree that we accept to have all that is false within us burned away. Then will we be enlightened and transfigured by His searing love. God wishes to consume the dross of our lives, to make us "light from light," fire from fire. He wishes to divinize us by sharing with us His very own nature (2 P 1:4).

St. John the Baptist bears witness to his surrendering act of love to God's Word: "He must grow greater, I must grow smaller. He who comes from above is above all others" (Jn 3:30-31). There is a necessary breaking of our independence so that God may break through with His saving Word. Charles Peguy in his poetical work, *Eve*, writes of this necessity of decreasing in order that God, the all-powerful One, may increase His power in us as He begins to transform us into images of His Divine Son:

> *You know that God alone gives of Himself,*
> *And that man's being unceasingly decreases...*
> *And that God's being unceasingly goes back*
> *To its eternal source and its deep night*

And of itself produces its own growth
And man's salvation and the world's strength.

Silence And Speech

WHEN WE ARE still, we can hear what the Other is saying in love through His Word. Silence and speech go together. It is like death and resurrection, martyrdom and transfiguration. We hear words and speak them in loneliness when we are not silent before the Lord. Silence becomes the womb in which God, as a Mother, brings us forth out of the infinite potentiality that lies within us by His infinite love-gift of Himself.

We express our humanity through communication. But our language, words and ideas must be conceived in inner silence. Silence helps us to purify and clarify our words. It enables us to discern clearly between what God is really saying to us and what we want to hear. How often do we claim the voice of God to be the echo of our own poor human thoughts.

We need to enter into the silence of Elijah. There, on the mount will we come to "hear" the begetting within us of God's Word. If our words are not enveloped in silence then we orphan our communication. Our words will lack true "parentage." They will not have been born of a knowledge of the Eternal Mother who begets all words in the One Word. If our speech breaks the life-line that attaches us to God's Word through inner silence and surrendering love, then only an emptiness — words spoken out of a void in our hearts — will come forth. We will be like lost ships in a stormy ocean without compass or propelling force to drive our message to the true haven of loving communication. We will be nothing more than "a gong booming or a cymbal clashing" (1 Cor 13:2). We will live on the destructive outer

rim of the hurricane rather than in the eye of God's calming
love.

We will treat more at length in another chapter the
purification that is involved in this dark night of surrender
that leads us into the light of the Lord's resurrection. But
first, like Elijah on Mount Horeb, we are being called to give
to God our undivided inner attention in a spirit of readiness
to serve and to do faithfully whatever God should ask of us.
We are to come aside and stand before the Lord in utter
emptiness but for the one burning desire: that He would
speak His Word to us as He spoke His Word to Samuel in the
temple: "Speak, Yahweh, your servant is listening" (1 S
3:11).

Your Word Is A Lamp

IF MOSES represents believers in adoration before the awesome God, Elijah symbolizes all who move to discover God
in the intimacy of their heart. "Happy the man who listens to
me, who day after day watches at my gates to guard the
portals" (Pr 8:34). We need, as in all true love affairs, to
experience the paradox that God is different from us and
yet He is not merely "another." He is not an object who looks
at us from outside and speaks words as human beings do. He
gazes at us from within at the core of our being. He calls us
each by our unique name in His eternal love (Is 43:1). And
from our center He speaks His Word to us in silence. We are
being created by His love in an ongoing process. We grow
into the fullness of our unique being the more we obey His
Word and observe His commands. "Now your word is a
lamp to my feet, a light on my path. . . Your decrees are my
- eternal heritage, they are the joy of my heart" (Ps 119:103,
111).

Romano Guardini well describes God as He gazes at us with eyes of love enabling us to become who we are in His eternal love:

God turns His face to man and thereby gives Himself to man. By looking at me He enables me to be myself. The soul lives in the loving gaze of God. This is an infinitely deep and blessed mystery. God is He who sees with the eyes of love by whose seeing things are enabled to be themselves, by whose seeing I am enabled to be myself (Living God).

Prayer is experiencing the intimate, creative, loving presence of God within us. He speaks not words, but His ever one Word in love. And He invites us to surrender totally to His creative love from within us as we discover that love in His silent Word. His speaking of His Word is a true begetting as a mother begets a child. Meister Eckhart, the 14th century Dominican mystic, speaks of the experience common to all mystics when they have entered into the "cave of the heart": "It may be asked whether this birth is best accomplished in man when he does the work and forms and thinks himself into God, or when he keeps himself in silence, stillness, and peace, so that God may speak and work in him. . . . The best and noblest way in which you may come into this work and life is by keeping silence and letting God work and speak. When all the powers are withdrawn from their work and images, there is this word spoken."

Holy Scripture speaks of God in terms of human attributes and attitudes. It is said in Scripture that God sees, knows, hears, listens and understands us. God protects and defends us. He forgives and has mercy on us. Elijah, on the mountain-top in the still, small voice, experienced God in a kind of intimate way that is normally characteristic of a child with his mother. In Hebrew the word often used by the sacred writers to express such a tender love, the motherly love which God has for us, is *Rabamim*, which is the plural of "maternal womb." Elijah covered his face with his cloak and withdrew into himself, overcome with adoration and with awe as he experienced this motherly love of God for him.

How often in the New Testament we read that Jesus looked with love at certain persons He encountered. His is the image of the look of God's motherly love for us in which we discover our true selves. In that look of love, God sees all our possibilities in His Word. He speaks that Word to us so that we can hear our names in that Word and surrender ourselves entirely to Him. Karl Rahner describes the type of deep, interior silence wherein we encounter our God:

> *If we are silent, if we forgive, if without reward we give ourselves wholeheartedly and are detached from ourselves, we are reaching out into a limitlessness which exceeds any assignable bound and which is nameless. We are reaching out towards the holy mystery which pervades and is the ground of our life. We are dealing with God* (Everyday Faith, p. 112).

As we enter into inner solitude, alone with the Alone who is God, we pray, "Yahweh Sabaoth, bring us back, let your face smile on us and we shall be safe" (Ps 80:7). With the eye of our spirit we gaze on God and experience His kenotic or emptying Love poured out in our hearts (Rm 5:5). In that solitude we become familiar with God's voice so that we can recognize it again when He speaks to us in the multiplicity of voices that surround us.

Solitude And Silence

IN A WORLD of ever increasing loneliness which has its own death-dealing silence, we need more solitude — a solitude that begets true silence, a centering solitude free of all exterior clamor and interior distraction, a solitude stripped of the desire to assert our false egos in lonely opposition and proud independence from the rest of the world.

Solitude differs from loneliness. Loneliness is the stage of a human being turning away from loving others to be locked into an inner prison where he or she morosely sits in dead, empty silence. It is like the black hole which is created, according to the latest hypothesis of the astronomers, when a star, having reached a certain mass-density, implodes upon itself and disappears, destroying itself in the process. True solitude, on the other hand, is always something positive. It touches God and allows us at the same time to be in purer touch with our own loved ones.

It is a paradox of solitude and silence that, whereas we appear to be absent from those we love in such a state, such physical absence develops in us a deeper spiritual union and loving presence to them than we could ever have imagined. Touching God in silence and solitude we touch other human beings, especially those we love the most, in new and deeper ways. There is a meeting of hearts in the heart of the one who is alone, especially consciously so, with the *Alone*.

Cardinal Newman described the Church as a home for solitary souls. It is the one Spirit of love who builds one Body with one Father over us all (Ep 4:4). When we have the courage to withdraw from our sinful habit of viewing reality only from our own narcissistic center, then we become productive members of the Body of Christ. His Spirit releases creative powers in us to live in self-sacrificing love for others. That is what it really means to be Church, to build the Body of Christ. Interestingly enough, as we move outward to communicate in love with others, our union with God increases. We all have experienced a special closeness with God in our loving service of others. Spinoza captured this idea when he wrote, "Our union with God increases in proportion to the growing realization of how many beings are united to Him in the same bond of love."

Love And Silence

IN THE BEAUTIFUL WORDS of the poet, Blessed Robert South-well, S.J., "Not where I breathe do I live, but where I love."This is the essential message of Christianity. ". . . as long as we love one another God will live in us and his love will be complete in us" (1 Jn 4:12). True love brings about a unique form of communication that unfolds in silence and solitude, an aloneness with God as the Alone who destroys all loneliness and brings us into the eternal community of divine love. Such love spans all distances of space and even time. In silence and solitude we can be present in love to all our loved ones wherever they may be. Even those who have died can be present to us in a deep communion of love when we have faith.

We see the power of silence to foster a deepening of relationships in the example of two lovers who have learned to communicate with one another wordlessly. Max Picard in his classic, *The World of Silence*, well describes this in these words:

> The words of lovers increase the silence. They only serve to make the silence audible. Only love can increase the silence by speaking. . .
> Lovers are the conspirators of silence. When a man speaks to his beloved, she listens more to the silence than to the spoken words of her lover. "Be silent," she seems to whisper. "Be silent that I may hear. . ."

Deep down at the core of our being there is in all of us a primordial silence. It is the spaceless space within, where

God silently whispers to us, "Pay attention, come to me; listen, and your soul will live" (Is 55:3). Our response should be similar to Elijah's gentle listening and quiet surrender to God, "Enough for me to keep my soul tranquil and quiet like a child in its mother's arms, as content as a child that has been weaned" (Ps 131:2). We need to discipline ourselves to calm the troubled waters of our heart. When we become centered in loving listening to God, we return to the beginning of all time when God spoke His Word in silence (Jn 1:1) and all things came forth.

We render our hearts silent, like a placid, motionless lake, so that God's Word, like a graceful swan, can glide effortlessly over it. Then the words which come forth from us, like the ripples formed by the dropping of a pebble on the waters, will bear God's message of love from us to who knows what far distant shore. In this primeval silence, each word of ours will be empowered by God's Word to reveal ever more the wonder of God's truth.

Yes, as the rain and the snow come down from the heavens and do not return without watering the earth, making it yield and giving growth to provide seed for the sower and bread for the eating, so the word that goes from my mouth does not return to me empty, without carrying out my will and succeeding in what it was sent to do (Is 55:10-11).

Broken Bread

ROOTED IN God's eternal silence and in inner solitude, we listen to God's Word. Christ again breaks bread for us as we spiritually join the disciples on the road to Emmaus or in the Upper Room and listen to Him say, "This is My Body, given for *you* unto life." In each moment there is a consecration of ourselves into God's Word and a recognition that both Christ and we are one.

Like Elijah when he heard God speak in the "still silent voice," and like the disciples at Emmaus, we rise from the table, strengthened by feeding on God's Word, to obey that Word. Elijah was rejuvenated by the experience of God in silence and replied, "I am filled with jealous zeal for Yahweh Sabaoth, because the sons of Israel have deserted you. . ." (1 K 19:14).

"Love does not come to an end" (1 Cor 13:8). Nor does the silence or the solitude which roots us in God's love. Instead, transformed by it, we rise and move out to serve others in obedience to the Word that God has spoken to us in our times of inner solitude and silence.

CHAPTER FOUR

The Silent Desert

CHRISTIANITY IS a religion built upon a desert spirituality. The historical exodus of the Israelites from their slavery in Egypt, through a 40-year period of purification in the Sinai Desert, to their eventual entrance into the Promised Land has become an archetype for all Christians. We, too, have been called by God from slavery to sin into our own inner desert, there to surrender to the purifying love and guidance of our heavenly Father for the entire course of our earthly existence. How easily we see ourselves in the stubbornness of the Israelites and their grumbling against God. We, too, cry out for living water and meat to eat (Ex 16:21). We, too, often yearn for a return to our unforgotten if shameful past of slavery and confinement and ask "Should we not do better to go back to Egypt?. . . Let us appoint a leader and go back to Egypt" (Nb 14:4).

God never forsakes His people. The only question is: How deeply into the desert of our own hearts do we wish to enter and there learn — by trial and tribulation, purification and testing — how to surrender to the supremacy of His love? Jesus, too, was led into the desert by the Holy Spirit (Mk 1:12) where He was forced to choose between the isolation of self-centered concerns and the true solitude of surrendering in love to the Father's providential care. All

His earthly life Jesus was tempted — as we are — but He never sinned (Heb 4:15). The desert experience was, for Him, a daily struggle between the power and plan of His heavenly Father and the lure and empty promises of evil as personified in the form of Satan. Often during His public life — following some thirty years of relative solitude in Nazareth — Jesus would retire into the desert, or other barren, quiet places, where He could be alone with the Father. He needed "connected aloneness" and "space" in which to experience His true self in His encounter with His loving Father as the Center of His being.

In His agony in the Garden of Gethsemane He struggled with the temptation that we all have to want to control our own lives. But He had triumphed over that temptation in the desert — and He did so here again — by surrendering complete control over His life to His heavenly Father: "Father, if you are willing, take this cup away from me. Nevertheless, let *your* will be done, not mine" (Lk 22:42-43). This struggle reached its apex as Jesus hung, suffering, on the cross that brought Him final death. Here He even felt abandoned by the Father and He cried out in His anguish, "*Eli, Eli, lama sabachthani?*" "My God, My God, why have you deserted me?" (Mt 27:46; Mk 15:34). Never before had He striven so to see the face of His Father again. Never before had He been so confronted with doubts about His mission, His Father's love for Him, His very own identity as the Son of God. Out of such apparent isolation, however, He was able to create a zone of silence and a sense of solitude. And it was thus that He was able to feel once more His oneness with His Father. It was this act of His will — this act of loving surrender in inner poverty — that resulted in His experiencing the fullness of the Father's love. Then filled with the Spirit of Love, He was able to peacefully and even joyfully commend His spirit to the Father and die (Lk23:46; Ps 31:6).

We are desert pilgrims also because we are followers of those early Christians who learned to enter into the desert of their hearts and by their faith, hope and love, consciously welcome the risen Lord who alone could conquer all the sin and evil in their lives. The desert Christians of the 4th century — following the example of the Israelites and indeed of Jesus Himself — were even led by the Spirit into the *physical* desert (which was merely a "place") where they could be reminded of the inner, desert place within their hearts. There they remained in solitude, advancing to new levels of oneness with Christ and with the entire world as they came in touch with Him, the Center of all reality, in whom God created all things.

Jesus often preached to His followers, including us in the 20th century, that, if we wanted to have a part of Him, we would have to deny ourselves, take up our cross each day and follow in His footsteps. That following will inevitably take us into the inner desert of our hearts where the battle between the forces of light and darkness is constantly taking place. Out of the aridity and emptiness of that desert God brings forth something new. He re-creates us in the image of His divine Son, sharing with us His own divine life: "And for anyone who is in Christ, there is a new creation; the old creation has gone, and now the new one is here" (2 Cor 5:17).

Seeking The Holy Grail

GOD HAS PUT within all of us not only a burning desire to become whole and integrated but also a burning thirst to become one with Him. Our entire life — whether we actually are aware or not of what we ultimately are seeking through our words and actions — is a journey in quest for such wholeness. Divided within ourselves as we are, we remain divided from others, from God and from the material world around us. The tragedy is we will always live "unreal," meaningless lives if we fail in our quest.

The medieval legend of the Holy Grail is a symbol of our search for inner integration. One version of this legend — which tells the story of the chalice used by Jesus at the Last Supper — was written centuries ago by Chrétien de Troyes. In his tale, the Holy Grail was kept in a castle in the care of a sovereign called the Fisher King. The king had been severely wounded in his adolescence and lay on a litter. In prophecy he was promised by the court jester that he would be healed by the Grail when an innocent fool came to the castle and asked him the right question. Parsifal was that fool. At some time or other most of us have probably read his story. It is the saga of a hero who wandered many years in search of the Holy Grail. He was told as a youth that if he asked the right question ("Whom does the Grail serve?"), he would find the Grail and be able to heal the king. But alas, when he met the king for the first time, the question went clean out of his mind. Nothing would bring it back. Then one day — it was Good Friday — Parsifal went to confession, was reconciled with God and the question came back to him. Once again, he set off for the castle, armed this time with the power to save the king. And here the story ends.

Throughout the ages authors have attempted to finish the tale. One attempt has Parsifal asking the right question — "Whom does the Grail serve?" — and hearing the answer: "It serves the Grail King." The sick king of the castle was healed at once. All his people lived in peace and joy while Parsifal was given the choicest room in the castle where he dwelt in splendor for the rest of his days.

Most of us live our lives in search of the Grail, in search of inner integration. We mistakenly see it as a goal which will bring us perfect happiness. And like Parsifal, we all too often forget to ask the right questions. The Grail, our inner integration, is not meant to serve our self-centered desires, our blinded values, our fruitless search for Paradise here on earth. When we set aside our own petty interests and pursuits — in the solitude away from our own clamorings for instant happiness as we conceive it — then we can learn how to ask the right questions. And in deep, surrendering silence, we will come to realize that the Grail, our inner integration, is meant to be used by us — not for ourselves but in the service of the King.

Inner Emptiness

A NUMBER of theologians of late have been referring to our modern age as a post-Christian epoch. Other writers believe it to be an age of "post-God." They don't want to declare with Nietzsche that "God is dead." But they wish to highlight that for the majority of human beings on the face of the earth, God, as a reality, does not enter into their everyday perceptions of life. For many, it is as if God's existence were a complete non-issue. It is as if He didn't really exist.

We, in our modern society have cut ourselves off from the experience of God as the ultimate Source and End of life. We have cut ourselves off, therefore, from the only source of perfect love and stability that we have and we are left floundering like oarsmen in a boat with no oars, buffeted by every storm and wave that toss us this way and that, like flotsam on the ocean. We are caught in the vice-grip of isolation. Entrapped within our own minds we look inward at nothing but a dark and meaningless void. We have built the prison. We are its prisoner. But we are also the jailer who holds the key but foolishly doesn't choose to open the door.

Strangely enough such self-inflicted isolation gives us a frantic craving for crowds of people to surround us. We throw ourselves into chaotic and noisy activities to drown out the bitter silence of our isolation. Yet we regard other human beings as competitors to be aggressively attacked or avoided by every possible evasive maneuver. In 1925, T.S. Eliot prophetically described so many of our con-temporaries who are living in this, the latter part of the 20th century, as

> . . . hollow men.
> We are the stuffed men
> Leaning together
> Headpiece filled with straw. Alas!
> Shape without form, shade without colour,
> Paralyzed force, gesture without motion   (The Hollow Men.)

Dr. Rollo May talks of the inner emptiness that exists in the hearts of many men when he writes:

> . . . the chief problem of people in the middle decade of the twentieth century is emptiness. By that I mean not only that many people do not know what they want; they often do not have any clear idea of what they feel. When they talk about lack of autonomy, or lament their inability to make decisions — difficulties which are present in all decades — it soon becomes evident that their underlying prob-lem is that they have no definite experience of their own desires or wants. Thus they feel swayed this way and that with painful feelings of powerlessness, because they feel vacuous, empty (Man's Search for Himself).

God, Where Are You?

BECAUSE we have cut ourselves off from God, we have only ourselves to cling to for strength. Opposed to God, we find ourselves cut off from our fellow human beings and also from all of nature around us. Jean Paul Sartre claims there is *no exit* from such absurdity. Hell, he says, is other people! And we can only stoically endure such destitution and meaninglessness. Still, there is a stirring among some today to go back home again and confess their brokenness, guilt and fear and to ask God's healing love to restore them to new life. Like St. Augustine, they have sought happiness outside and are now returning within themselves to search for the Source of their happiness Who dwells therein.

> *Too late have I loved Thee, O Thou, Beauty of ancient days, yet ever new! Too late have I loved Thee! And behold, Thou wert within and I abroad, and there I searched for Thee, deformed, I plunging amid those fair forms which Thou hast made. Thou wert with me, but I was not with Thee, which unless they were in Thee, were not at all* (Confessions, X, 27).

Others, unfortunately, seek — through mind-expanding drugs, parapsychology or Far-Eastern religions — to unlock the inner genie that will solve all their problems and guarantee them sudden bliss and perfect happiness. Some are turning to Christianity to find in a fundamentalistic literal interpretation of the Bible the source of their security. The charismatic renewal has opened up for others a freshness in their approach to God's love in the meaningful religious experience of being "born again" in the Spirit. The great question, though, still remains: How deep into the desert do we wish to go? Many Christians replace one static form of religious belief, ritual or piety with another. Only the name changes, for there has not been the desire to stay in the desert and fight the battle between isolation and true solitude, between the darkness of self-centeredness and the light of God's indwelling Word.

Eastern Christianity

STILL OTHER CHRISTIANS are rediscovering their roots which take them back to early Christianity as it evolved out of Semitic and patristic spirituality. The earliest Christians lived "theology" as a life in the risen Christ. This gave them a new integration through their simple obedience to the message of the Gospel of loving God with the very love of God's Spirit within them (Rm 5:5) and loving each human being in his or her unique personhood, created and loved individually by the triune God. In the midst of paganism, the followers of Christ gave witness to the "good news" that Jesus Christ is God become man who died out of passionate love for each of us. Such early Christians believed by faith that Christ rose from the dead and lived victoriously within them. No sin or evil had any control or power over them any more.

Yet they realized as they lived in the aloneness with the Alone that there were obstacles, demonic powers working within them to destroy this divine life within and around them in the world. The theology of living redemption or inner healing was developed — not by abstract thinkers, but by men and women who in the 4th century fled literally, into the Egyptian desert. There they took up the attack and eliminated the "worldliness," the lure of evil forces, and the power of darkness from their hearts and thus from the material world around them.

The dominant tone of their spirituality was one of aggression. The darkened prisons where Christians of the first three centuries wasted away, the amphitheaters where voracious beasts tore the martyrs apart, were replaced by the immense deserts of sand and sterility and by inner psychic deserts of darkness and aridity. For them the desert became the symbol of the twilight zone between the profane world that groaned under the bondage of sin or chaotic disorientation from God and the heavenly Jerusalem of the transfigured world to come.

They did not run away from the physical world in cowardliness or in self-centered spiritual egoism. Rather, they were conscious co-creators, fighters at the most advanced outposts, "men intoxicated with God" (as Pseudo-Macarius calls them). They were desert prophets, building a community, a way of life with God that most closely would resemble the life to come in the *eschaton*. Although living in a body in time and space, they pointed to a transfigured, spiritual existence outside of time and space which they were beginning to experience as the "really real" world within them. It was returning to the Garden of Eden, to an inner and outer harmony between themselves and God, with other beings and with all nature.

By entering into themselves, these ascetics sought by God's grace to fructify the seeds of divinity sown in them when God decreed freely to create them according to His own image and likeness. These early desert pilgrims sought chiefly to experience in the deepest recesses of their heart, mind and soul the love and presence of the living, loving Trinity. They expressed with their lives the conviction that it was ultimately necessary to go apart from the world to find God in the solitude of constant prayer and inner, austere attentiveness over every thought and imagination, as St. Paul wrote (2 Cor 10:5).

The risen Lord was the center of their lives. Like St. Paul, they wanted to be co-crucified with Christ so that they would live no longer they themselves but Christ would dominate their every thought, word and deed (Gal 2:20). They yearned with all their heart and soul to be consumed by Him. No price was too great to pay. They were mystics, seekers of God in the truest sense of the word and, there fore, they were willing to surrender all and everything in order to experience greater love and union with Him and service in love to their neighbors. Into the dry, barren wasteland they went, these mad, passionate lovers of Christ, these Christians intoxicated with God. They hoped and believed that in the deadness of the sterile desert which lay inside their heart they would be given Life. They entered this desert that they might be transformed into a new creation as their former, false selves were put to death, as they learned to silence the noises in their heart to listen and obey the living Word of God spoken in the depths of their very being.

Hesychasm

THE FATHERS of the desert developed a spirituality they called *hesychasm*. It comes from the Greek word, *hesychia*, which means tranquility or inner peace. Today we could call it integration or, to quote Carl Jung's term, the process of "individuation." It is a movement which, through constant ascetical practices and vigilance over every thought, brought the Christian out of lonely isolation and self-centeredness to a new state of solitude where God was revealed as the Source of all life and the ultimate concern of the individual. This solitude paradoxically brought about the inner silence that is the language of love.

St. Arsenius has always been considered the model of a true *hesychast*. Such a spirituality describes the Christian through grace and individual intense asceticism, reintegrating his or her whole being into a single "self" that is then placed completely under the direct influence of God dwelling within. Such integration comes only with continued efforts on the part of the individual to silence all parts of his or her being. In an "aloneness" with the indwelling Trinity that person can "hear" God speak His living Word. In such integrative silence and by God's grace one finds the power to obey in complete and loving submission.

Arsenius, as the story is told in the *Lives of the Fathers*, while still at the imperial court of Constantinople, prayed to God in these words: "Lord, lead me along a way to life where I can be saved." A voice said to him: "Arsenius, flee men and you will be saved." The same Arsenius, now a hermit, in his new lifestyle reiterated his same prayer and he again heard a voice reply to him saying, "Arsenius, flee, keep silence, remain tranquil; these are the roots of inpeccability."

Withdrawal

WHOEVER ASPIRES to attain this most intimate union with God must imitate the Israelites who fled from the Egyptians into the desert where they met God as their only Source of happiness. Among the early hermits, as St. Anthony taught, such physical removal from the many temptations and cares of the world was considered as the first condition to attain purity of heart. Exterior and interior silence, in the words of St. Basil, is the beginning of purity of heart. Withdrawal from the world would make no sense unless there was an inner withdrawal from attachments to persons, places and things that impede a total attachment solely to the indwelling God.

St. John Climacus talks of the inner solitude which results from withdrawal from all preoccupation with creatures in order to focus one's attention on God:

> *The beginning of solitude is to throw all noise off as disturbing for the depth of the soul. And the end of it is not to fear disturbances and to remain insusceptible to them. Though going out, yet without a*

*word, he is kind and wholly a house of love. He is not easily moved
to speech, nor is he moved to anger. The opposite of this is obvious*
(Ladder of Divine Ascent, *Step 27, 5*).

St. John Climacus further defines silence as, first, detachment from concern with regard to all things, necessary
and unnecessary; second, as assiduous prayer; and third, as
the unremitting action of prayer in the heart. Silence does
not come easily to us in our day and age. Living in our
modern world, we cannot easily run away from the "world,"
the physical world where most of us live and work and play.
But our inner desert of banality and boredom as we go about
our daily tasks, the desert of loneliness that comes over all of
us even when we are among our loved ones but do not feel
that we are one with them, the desert of meaninglessness or
senselessness that confronts so much that happens to us or
surrounds us in our world, all call us to a certain withdrawal.
This is not an escape in a physical sense so much as it is an
inner turning in solitude to meet God at our center.

It is a true withdrawal from the senseless dissipation of
our inner energies and a movement into our true self that is
discovered only by a "return" unto ourselves. It is an avoid-
ance of the evasionary tactics which our false egos call for in
order to avoid confrontation with our true self in Christ.
What strength it takes at times to be honest with ourselves
and come aside awhile to rest and — in silence — hear God's
Word! On the contrary, any temptation to remain in isolation, which is a pseudo-solitude and the opposite of true,
loving listening and surrendering to God's Word, leads to
self-centeredness and away from true communication with
God and neighbor in love.

Keep Silence

THE SILENCE taught by the hesychastic fathers and which is so important for us to learn first refers to physical silence and the exercise of stringent control over our tongue. But it goes further and encourages us to a deeper, inner silence of all within us that causes "noise" or impediments to our listening to God. Silence becomes an inner "space" where we are able to experience the silent presence of God. This is more than a mere passive waiting for God, a pause before God does something. It is the active concentration of one's whole being, moving beyond any pre-conditioning, prejudices, fears or other psychic bondage into a state of passionate indifference and burning desire to encounter the Lord and to listen to Him speak, wordlessly and without images.

And He does speak! The Christian experiences His Word as healing, comforting, filling the individual with peace and joy, giving counsel, knowledge and understanding beyond mere human reasoning. It is not so much a dialogue of ideas or answers to questions. It is a coming into a oneness with the Lord wherein God's love is received in the person of Jesus Christ and a corresponding response is given on the level of one's unique personhood.

Such inner silence is part of a continued conversion, a turning away from self-centeredness, the spirit of the world, noise and confusion, and becoming God-centered by entering into the spirit of Jesus and the silence of love. It is a coming home and discovering our oneness with the mind of Christ as St. Paul encourages us all: "Your mind must be renewed by a spiritual revolution so that you can put on the new self that has been created in God's way, in the goodness and holiness of the truth" (Ep 4:23-24).

Remain Tranquil

THIS IS much more than "keeping your cool!" This is entering into God's seventh day rest. This is the state called *apatheia* by the Fathers of the desert. St. Augustine defined peace as "the tranquility of order." Apatheia is the state of integration or self-control whereby we allow the grace of God to filter down into our hearts to be the sole determinant of all our actions. We no longer act without reflection. True love has conquered the heart and we wait calmly to see what line of action or thought will be most "loving" toward God who has so completely loved us into being. Only those who have control of all their inordinate passions can act constantly in such a virtuous manner by living totally under the virtue or power of Jesus. It is the state that Teilhard de Chardin describes as "passionate indifference."

Through vigorous inner attentiveness to anything from without that might move us to vanity or pride, we enter into a reintegration of our whole being: senses, emotions, intellect and will. We become rooted in God in tranquility, a peaceful resting in Him which is very dynamic in that it is always seeking the good pleasure of the Lord. This is far removed from any self-centered quietism. It is a return to Eden and the restoration of man and woman in Christ, the fulfillment of God's plan to make man and woman according to the image and likeness of God that is Jesus Christ. It is entering into the true freedom of sons and daughters of a loving Father. It is sharing in the fullness of life that Jesus came to bring us (Jn 10:10). This is active receptivity in which God can ask anything of us and we joyfully respond to do His will.

Thomas Merton well grasps this desert silence that brings inner tranquility:

*All the paradoxes about the contemplative way are reduced to this
one: being without desire means being led by a desire so great that it
is incomprehensible. . . It is a blind desire, which seems like a desire
for "nothing" only because nothing can content it. . . But true
emptiness is that which transcends all things, and yet is immanent
in all. For what seems to be emptiness in this case is pure being. It is
not this, not that. . . The character of emptiness, at least for a
Christian contemplative, is pure love, pure freedom. Love that is
free of everything, not determined by any thing or held down by any
special relationship. It is love for love's sake. It is a sharing,
through the Holy Spirit, in the infinite charity of God. . . This
purity, freedom and indeterminateness of love is the very essence of
Christianity* (The Climate of Monastic Prayer, *p. 128*).

Darkness Before The Dawn

BUT BEFORE we can come into the Promised Land of transforming love and deepest union with God, there is so much
desert yet to be traversed. There are so many excruciating
sufferings and inner purifications which we must undergo.
We may wonder what applications this chapter on *desert
silence* may have for us in our spiritual journey. God, the
Divine Physician, knows each one of us to be unique. He
knows what needs to be silenced in our hearts, one so different from another. Yet from the common teaching of the
great Christian mystics, we can learn what awaits us if we
only have the courage to continue our march through our
own inner deserts.

Sometimes we are led into the battle of the desert outside
ourselves. When our friends and loved ones express their
love by affirming us in word and deed, we praise God for
such gifts. But what happens when we receive snubs, cold-
ness, suspicion, calumnies and detractions, not only from
"enemies," but above all from our own friends? Such occasions make us confront the hidden areas of unresolved

pride within ourselves. The *Imitation of Christ* expresses it
well in terms of desert spirituality:

> *It is good for us now and then to have some troubles and ad-*
> *versities; for often times they make a man enter into himself, that he*
> *may know that he is an exile, and place not his hopes in anything of*
> *this world. It is good for us sometimes to suffer contradictions and to*
> *allow people to think ill and slightingly of us, even when we do and*
> *mean well. These are often helps to humility, and rid us of vain*
> *glory. For then we more earnestly seek God to be witness of what*
> *passes within us, when outwardly we are slighted by men, and*
> *incur their discredit (Book 1, ch. 12).*

We should be convinced that there can be no true integration of all our powers into a consistent, authentic, loving
true self unless there is humility. And there can be no
humility unless the false ego in us is put to death through
humiliations. The "best" humiliations are those which arise
in a natural way within the context of our very human
situation. The desert in which we find ourselves provides the
scene of the conflict.

And the most intense sufferings will come to us when we
are utterly convinced that we have been loving to others and
in return receive only indifference or abuse. In the very
name of following Jesus more perfectly we set ourselves up
often times for the inner battle to take place. Our very love
of Christ may well provide the cause for our suffering of
rebukes and humiliations. Often good and loving fellow-
Christians — perhaps the local pastor, members of our
family or religious community, persons with whom we normally pray together — become occasions for greater purifications. But did not Jesus pronounce a special blessing on us
in such circumstances?

Happy those who are persecuted in the cause of right: theirs is the kingdom of heaven. Happy are you when people abuse you and persecute you and speak all kinds of calumny against you on my account. Rejoice and be glad for your reward will be great in heaven; this is how they persecuted the prophets before you (Mt 5:10-12).

St. Paul also exhorts us to the reality that we will be called to suffer for the sake of Christ: "You are well aware, then, that anybody who tries to live in devotion to Christ is certain to be attacked" (2 Tm 3:13). As we accept such adversities from others in a loving and joyful spirit and in union with the suffering Lord, we begin to see them, not as merely negative forces operating against us, but rather as steps to a new transformation into Christ. After some experience of the healing that results through the therapy of suffering humiliations from others, we can actually reach a point where we praise God for such happenings as we begin to perceive how this or that suffering contains the will of God inside it, and how He is guiding us to greater gentleness and humility through it. We may never *like* such sufferings, but we can experience the blessings that flow from them when we abandon ourselves to let Jesus be Lord in such occasions. We can exercise in such happenings the faith-filled words of St. Paul: "We know that by turning everything to their good God cooperates with all those who love him, with all those that he has called according to his purpose" (Rm 8:28).

Mid-Life Crises

THERE ARE certain humiliations which diminish us in our own self-esteem and which we suffer "passively." They come to us not only from without but also from within. And these are humiliations that we don't necessarily bring about but which happen to us along our journey in the desert of life. Such things as sickness, the loss of a loved one through death, or the gradual breakdown of the powers of our body and psyche diminish us and are necessarily a part of our journey to that greatest dissolution in our final physical death. All of us undergo physical, psychological and spiritual struggles in the transitions which bring us in a dramatic way to that final struggle with the laughing specter who will reveal himself one day to us as Death.

Middle age for most of us is a period of our life when in our inner desert we come face to face with the reality that we are slowing down in many ways. Death begins to leer at us and taunt us with reminders that we will not live forever on this earth. No one escapes indefinitely. Death will come to you just as it will come to me. About that there is no doubt! Transitional points — little occasions in which we are forced to "die to self" — help to prepare us for the bigger struggles which can lead us unto greater "glory" or throw us into even greater darkness and negativity.

We can seek to escape these encounters with death before the final call to die. We can throw ourselves into even greater activity. To avoid the silence of our growing impotence on many levels, we paradoxically move into isolation farther away from our true self and enter into a greater loneliness. Yet our frenetic activities and our bravado attempts to escape death as though everything were normal remove us from the desert struggle to which the Lord is calling us. Like the Israelites who refused to go farther into the desert under God's guiding hand and who refused to surrender to His loving providence there, we seek to go backwards to a level of greater "security." We want to go back to Egypt but that only brings us back into slavery.

Such transitional times in our life offer us opportunities of great healing and the deepening of our faith, hope and

love. We can stay, as the Fathers of the desert exhort us, in
our "cell" and wage our inner battle manfully. We can
accept lovingly from God's hands such diminishments and
transform them into growth experiences in our radical de-
pendency and complete abandonment to God who alone
knows and controls the time and circumstances of our ultimate departure from this world. Each reminder that we are
not really God but that we are His beloved children, made by
Him to share in His very own life for eternity, builds trust in
our hearts that God is indeed merciful and wise and, above
all that His infinite power can and will bring out of the
aridity of our desert situation a new creation, a new life out
of the "death" we are experiencing. The prophet Isaiah well
expresses what our Christian hope should be as we accept
this dying process: "He will destroy Death forever. The
Lord Yahweh will wipe away the tears from every cheek" (Is
25:8).

Death, Where Is Your Sting?

WE TRULY DIE as we live. Those who have lived by deep faith,
hope and love will die in such virtues. The childlike spirit of
abandonment will be operative in that ultimate "letting-go."
The peace and joy of the Holy Spirit that filled their earthly
pilgrimage in times of adversities will flood them in abun-
dance on their deathbed. Such a Christian has daily said with
St. Paul, "I face death every day" (1 Cor 15:3). We learn to
fear no adversity, not even final death itself, for by daily
abandoning our desires to those of God's holy will, we know
that nothing in life or death can ever separate us from the
love of Christ (Rm 8:38).

All through our earthly pilgrimage in the many desert
experiences we have undergone — all to reach their climax
in our ultimate passage from this earth — we enjoy a blessed

security, stability and certitude, not in our own power or merits but in God's infinite love for us. In life and in death, while still in our corruptible bodies, we already experience something of the immortality, incorruptibility and unchangeability of God's eternal love for us. Death in any form has no sting, no victory over us, because we have learned to battle with each death-dealing situation. We have put to death something of our false-egos in each such struggle in order to live positively in the victory of Jesus (1 Cor 15:54-57). And we know that many more intense struggles from within await us before we reach that final moment of dissolution.

The Dark Night

NO PERSECUTIONS or trials that come to us from the outside can ever compare to the inner purifications that we must undergo in order to reach that point of integration where we are — in every thought, word and deed — completely surrendered to God. The great Christian mystics, the advance scouts in the desert of life, liken such inner purifications of the senses and the inner faculties of soul and spirit to a struggle in the darkest of nights against inner adversaries that can be likened only to an experience of descending into hell itself.

Such purifications admit of many degrees of intensity. But we can readily believe from Christ's teaching that the Father purifies and prunes those whom He loves in order that they may bring forth greater fruit (Jn 15:2). All true "athletes" of the desert know that love of God and neighbor is proved by deeds. We can actively suffer in loving service toward others. But the most important sufferings are not those we do, but those we undergo by God's more direct involvement. He knows, as our Divine Physician, how to purify those deep roots within us that tie us in a collective unconscious back through our ancestry to the first man and woman. He takes away the scaffolding we needed in earlier periods of our prayer-life. He "hides" His presence that we so lovingly experienced in His consolations and in the many beautiful insights He used to give us.

One of the great masters of dark night purifications is St. John of the Cross. He gives us the reason why God, in His great love for us, takes away from us His consolations and leads us into a deeper purification of our senses and spirit:

> *It should be known, then, that God nurtures and caresses the soul, after it has been resolutely converted to His service, like a loving mother who warms her child with the heat of her bosom, nurses it with good milk and tender food, and carries and caresses it in her arms. But as the child grows older, the mother withholds her caresses and hides her tender love; she rubs bitter aloes on her sweet breast and sets the child down from her arms, letting it walk on its own feet so that it may put aside the habits of childhood and grow accustomed to greater and more important things* (The Dark Night, *Bk. 1, ch. 1*).

We are being called by God to love Him solely for Himself and not for His gifts. Deeper into our hearts we plunge and there find more of the aridity of the desert and the dry bones of our own weaknesses. We see ourselves with renewed displeasure as areas deep within us are opened up revealing the intensity of the "sin" that still resides within. St. John of the Cross well describes our call to more intense purification:

> *. . . God divests the faculties, affections and senses, both spiritual and sensory, interior and exterior. He leaves the intellect in darkness, the will in aridity, the memory in emptiness and the affections in supreme affliction, bitterness and anguish, by depriving the soul*

*of the feeling and satisfaction it previously obtained from spiritual
blessings. For this privation is one of the conditions required that
the spiritual form, which is the union of love, may be introduced in
the spirit and united with it. The Lord works all of this in the soul by
means of a pure and dark contemplation* (The Dark Night, *Bk.
2, ch. 2*).

Bittersweet

SUCH AN INNER NIGHT where there is no longer any light
from our own intellectual powers to guide us, no consolations to strengthen us, seems very dense and dark indeed.
Everything around us in our inner desert seems so dry and
empty. We feel that we will never find God again; and yet
there comes over us no true panic or disquietude. There is
only a deep abiding trust that God will come; that, in a way,
He is present in His seeming absence. We are being called by
God into a new aloneness with Him, into a deeper silencing
of all our desires to live in the stillness of complete surrender
to let Him do in our life whatever it is He wishes. Silence is
no longer a thing we seek but it is becoming a part of our
very makeup. We are *becoming* a "silence," persons totally
receptive to God at all times in our daily living. We are
becoming contemplatives, listening to God's Word at all
times. We are learning how to pray incessantly.

We find ourselves listening and ready to follow God's
call: "That is why I am going to lure her and lead her out into
the wilderness and speak to her heart" (Ho 2:16). No longer
are we experiencing God through our own thoughts or
feelings that register so strongly in our senses. Now we live
in the rarefied atmosphere of purer faith, greater abandonment to God to let Him speak His Word as He wishes. We
have no desires now but one magnificent obsession: to let
God have His loving way in our life. We come to know God

by not knowing, in the cloud of unknowing. Yet we are knowing Him in a deeper way. He is penetrating deeper into our hearts, becoming Lord of their every thought or desire. We are expanding our consciousness of those dark potentialities of our subconscious and declaring that this part of the desert is now under the reign of God.

We feel immobile, blocked at the bottom of the mountain, completely alone. We cry out to see the face of God. We experience our own creatureliness, inner poverty and utter dependence upon Him. If He does not answer our plea and come to our rescue, we feel we will surely perish. The enemies are all around us. There is no avenue of escape from what seems to be imminent death. God is becoming our sole strength. Truly, to become a contemplative — to become integrated in all our body, soul and spirit relationships under God's love — demands the greatest suffering.

The darkness that invades the mind fills us with repugnance, disgust and an interior revolt. We want to run away from the narrowing experiences of the desert. We want to break the silence by the noises of diversions, by the pleasures of the senses. The revolt registers itself in the lower part of our consciousness, something like that felt by Jesus in the Garden (Lk 22:42). We have the impression that we can do nothing, as though we were sinking ever deeper into quicksand. We are totally deprived of any power to extricate ourselves from the dark pit into which we have fallen. Still in our higher powers of intellect and will, permeated by a purer faith, a more complete hope, we are able to acknowledge a purified love of God. We struggle on, surrendering ourselves to the free operation of God's grace in our spiritual lives. With no sensible fervor felt and a deep awareness of our own weaknesses, failings and limitations, we enter into an interior battle of flesh and violent temptations which add to the growing conviction that we have fallen from fidelity to God. We believe that God despises us in our sinfulness and that we will never be pleasing to Him again.

To stay in the desert and engage in the battle with these temptations, to strive to be faithful, to seek God's light and a way out of the turmoil, only heighten the anguish felt. And yet patience and fortitude rooted in deep humility and trust in God must be exercised. It is here that one's abandonment to God in such interior trials must also be manifested in perfect obedience and trust to the guidance of one's spiritual director. Hopefully such a spiritual director will be enlightened — both from his or her own experience in advanced contemplation and from the study of mystical theology and the writings of the great Christian mystics — not to insist that such trials are always the result of sin or necessarily come from other natural causes such as laziness, tepidity and melancholy. The value of such purifications is that they bring about a new oneness in a more total surrender of oneself to the sovereignty of God. He is becoming our one, true God and we are beginning to fulfill the great *shema*, the great command to love God with our whole heart, our whole soul, our whole mind and all our strength (Dt 6:6).

Reintegration

As WE LEARN to surrender to God's complete control on all levels of our being, we begin to experience a silencing of such noise as comes from the disharmony among the various parts of our being. We enter and remain in that void, that inner emptiness of all that may impede us from being totally surrendered to God's Spirit of love. We live by what the prophet Isaiah wrote:

> *Let anyone who fears Yahweh among you*
> *listen to the voice of His servant!*
> *Whoever walks in darkness,*
> *and has no light shining for him,*
> *let him trust in the name of Yahweh,*
> *let him lean on his God (Is 50:10).*

The desert is the path that leads us into a new life in God. We are approaching the Promised Land of mystical oneness with God. We are returning home, to our true state, to a consciousness of being in Christ. The many layers and layers of psychical and spiritual obstacles, that have accumulated within our consciousness and subconscious through heredity and faulty education, our own failures and sins, the actions and reactions of others upon our character, have obscured the real image of Christ according to which we have been created. He has always been speaking His loving, healing, transforming words from within but the noises we have allowed to take over have drowned out that still, silent Voice. Purifications have begun to remove the obstacles. The features of Christ, the great Icon of the Father's love for us, are returning to their original brightness and brilliance.

St. Gregory of Nyssa expresses what is happening as we become more integrated into Christ:

> *Now the removal of what is foreign is a return to what is con-*
> *natural and fitting; and this we can only achieve by becoming what*
> *we once were in the beginning when we were created. Yet to achieve*
> *this likeness to God is not within our power nor within any human*
> *capacity. It is a gift of God's bounty, for He directly bestowed this*
> *divine likeness on our human nature at its creation* (Homily on
> the Canticle of Canticles, *XV*).

Renewing The World

THE PARADOX of desert silence that brings the individual so completely into the deepest union with the Trinity is never really only vertically related. Rainer Maria Rilke expresses the value of solitude as opening us up to the world around us: "Love your solitude for through it you will begin to have grace to see clearly about you." Jesus taught this paradox that, if we were to lose our life, our false ego and pass over into the freedom of the children of God by obeying His commands, we would not only find our true life but we would find that such a true self can only be one with God, nature and all other human beings. God created all persons and things to be in harmony, each a part of the whole and each containing the whole.

As we move away from our isolated false self to discover what we truly are in our identity through God's love, God's Spirit reveals to us that all other human beings have been created uniquely beautiful and to be loved both by God and by ourselves in that inner beauty that is theirs. The quiet and calm that have come to us as we center upon the infinite love of God dwelling within us bring us into a similar quiet, calm and receptivity toward the persons who surround us. No longer are they digits, impersonalized things, objects. Having contacted our real self within, we can now make contact with the real self in others. There can be no true love toward others without an equally true love for God and for ourselves experienced in solitude when we are alone with God as Center.

Only when we experience our own inner beauty before God are we empowered to "appropriate" that self and give it as a personalized gift of love in service to those around us. Touching God, we touch all of God's creatures, especially those closest to us who, like us, have been made according to

God's image and likeness and for whom Jesus died. We see how a loving community is brought about when we put on the nuptial mindset of Jesus Christ toward those closest to us. Friendships, especially in marriage, have to be rooted in solitude and inner silence if each is to love the other as God loves them. This is what St. Paul holds out as the Christian ideal: "Husbands should love their wives just as Christ loved the Church and sacrificed himself for her to make her holy" (Ep 5:25).

A Loving Presence To Others

IN SOLITUDE we touch God and experience His total presence to us as "availability," "mutuality," and "I-Thou," and a "self-gifting" to us in His Son and Spirit. Only to the degree that such godly love has been experienced profoundly in the depths of our being can we become a loving presence to others. For to become available in an I-Thou relationship of equals who share in the mutual gift of each other we must realize our own inner beauty. We must be conscious of the gift we wish to make of ourselves. We must be in possession of that gift. This means that all death-dealing elements that come out of isolation must be done away with if a transformation of our true self is to ever take place.

St. Maximus the Confessor builds a theology called *Logos* mysticism on this concept. Once we have become purified through asceticism, we are able in the purity of our hearts to see God everywhere operating in each creature, in each event, through His creative Logos. It is to discover the unique logos or inner relationship to the Logos and in the Logos to God in the total plan of His creation. He writes:

> *Then man sees all things in God first as flowing from God into existence and secondly through them, rising to God as to the end of*

*all moved creatures and the fixed and stable ground of their being,
who is the end of every rule and law, the end of every word and
mind and of every nature, the infinite and unbound goal of all
beings* (Ambigua).

Teilhard de Chardin beautifully summarizes the power
of love: "Love differentiates as it unites" (*Phenomenon of
Man*). Christianity is a religion rooted in the love of God that
transforms us into living members of the Body of Christ, the
Church. There can be no separation between solitude and
aloneness with God and a similar solitude shared with each
person we meet. Contemplation is love in action. The more
we die to the elements in our total make-up that impede a
higher mode of being toward others, the greater transforming love we can release in the world. The more we can do —
by exercising our faith in God's loving and energizing presence in our lives and through our work — to fashion the
Body of Christ, the more alive we will become. We will seek
to surrender ourselves to God's infinite power within us and
within the moment, and experience freeing love in every
action that we perform in the awareness of our union with
Him in our work.

Return To Eden

THE BOOK of Genesis describes how man and woman were
created to enjoy a very special kind of intimacy with God
(Gn 3:8) and a oneness in harmony with all the created
world in an ongoing process of creative work performed in
love and not in selfishness. But sin entered and the desert of
sterility and chaos, disharmony and dissension replaced
God's view of reality. Man and woman became self-centered
and not God-centered. They were no longer living in the
silence of true love to build a greater oneness between

themselves and the rest of the world. Instead, they hid in the narrowness of the prison created by their own self-love. They forgot the universal language of love which spaced its words with silence. In their isolation, the noise which reigned in their hearts drowned out the *Logos* of God. But to those who have the courage to be still and know that God is their God, their loving Father (Ps 46:10), God gives the experience, promised by Him, of a new creation.

> *But Yahweh your God is bringing you into a prosperous land, a land of streams and springs, of waters that well up from the deep in valleys and hills, a land of wheat and barley, of vines, of figs, of pomegranates, a land of olives, of oil, of honey, a land where you will eat bread without stint, where you will want nothing, a land where the stones are of iron, where the hills may be quarried for copper. You will eat and have all you want and you will bless Yahweh your God in the rich land he has given you (Dt 8:8-10).*

This is the logic of love and the language of the desert. Death not only brings us to life, but death is already new life when it is death to selfishness and isolation. The desert silence teaches us — once we have allowed God to crash down our created idols, even if they are made of gold — that God has always been speaking His saving Word, Jesus Christ. He has always been standing at the door of our heart knocking that we might open it and allow Him to enter into our lives (Rv 3:20). The desert, above all, is the place within our hearts where God becomes our loving Father as we silence all our own efforts to create reality according to our own image. We surrender to God in true solitude whose language is silence. In such silence we offer back to God, who has given us all things in His Son, Jesus Christ, the gift of our very selves.

The real question is still: How far down into our hearts, into the desert within, do we wish to go? Are we dissatisfied with living only around the fringes of the oasis where we find our security in things and not in God alone? Do we really believe that God can bring out of the sterility of the desert a new and fertile land? Do we believe that if we die to our false self and live in God's Spirit we can enter into that new creation that is always measured by our greater oneness with Christ and oneness with the whole world, all of nature, created in God's Word, and with every man and woman made, like us, according to God's image and likeness? The beautiful ode of the poet, Francis Thompson, well expresses why Christianity is built on a desert spirituality:

> *For there is nothing lives but something dies,*
> *And there is nothing dies but something lives.*
> *Till skies be fugitives,*
> *Till Time, the hidden root of change, updries,*
> *Are Birth and Death inseparable on earth;*
> *For they are twain yet one, and death is Birth.*
>
> (Ode to a Setting Sun).

CHAPTER FIVE

The Silence Of Jesus

LOVE IN SILENCE is always incomplete until it is enfleshed in a surrendering word that says, "I love you." Such a word, however is spoken, as we have seen, out of silence and continues in silence to be lived out effectively by self-surrendering action. God Himself sets the example: "For upright is the word of the Lord and all His works are trustworthy" (see Ps 33:4-9). He is a self-giving Father who, wishing even greater intimacy with the chosen Israelites of old, pitched His active presence in the Tent of the Meeting (Ex 33:7). When Solomon built the Temple on Mount Zion, God took up His abode there, remaining in loving silence among His people. As they turned toward Jerusalem, the Jews knew God was there, listening and answering their prayers.

How the faithful Jews longed to stand in silence in the courts of Yahweh's Temple:

> *. . . a single day in your courts*
> *is worth more than a thousand elsewhere,*
> *merely to stand on the steps of God's house*
> *is better than living with the wicked (Ps 84:10).*

But God wished to communicate Himself still more intimately and more completely to the world by giving it an indisputable sign of His love. The central point of all human history is the Incarnation when God pitched His tent among us in the temple of the human body of Jesus the Messiah.

> *When peaceful silence compassed everything and the night in its swift course was half spent, down from the heavens, from the royal throne leaped your all powerful Word; into the heart of a doomed land the fierce warrior leapt (Ws 18:14-15).*

As silently as God spoke His Word and the world of so many creatures gently came forth into being, so God in silence brought forth His Word made flesh in His birth from Mary in a cave at Bethlehem. Christian piety, with a wisdom from God, has always associated Christ's birth with the symbols of external silence. There was no room for them in the inn where the noise of revelers and worldly minded people would surely have disturbed their peace. In the solitude of a hillside cave, He was born in a stable where He was close to nature and surrounded by the animals of the field. An angel announced His birth to shepherds who were quietly tending their sheep nearby: "Today in the town of David a saviour has been born to you; he is Christ the Lord. And here is a sign for you: you will find a baby wrapped in swaddling clothes and lying in a manger" (Lk 2:11-12).

He who blankets the heavens with the sun, the moon and the stars was wrapt in a flimsy swaddling cloth. He cried for His mother's milk, He who feeds the entire world. He reached out for the warm embrace of his foster father whose arms embrace the universe. Right from His first appearance in our midst, God's Word made flesh shows us that "God's foolishness is wiser than human wisdom, and God's weakness is stronger than human strength" (1 Cor 1:25).

God's Silent Word

JESUS IS the definitive Word of God in person. Who hears Him, hears the Father; who sees Him, sees the Father (Jn 14:9). Everything that God has spoken through His creative Word is fulfilled in Him.

> *At various times in the past and in various different ways, God spoke to our ancestors through the prophets; but in our own time, the last days, he has spoken to us through his Son, the Son that he has appointed to inherit everything and through whom he made everything there is. He is the radiant light of God's glory and the perfect copy of his nature, sustaining the universe by his powerful command; and now that he has destroyed the defilement of sin, he has gone to take his place in heaven at the right hand of divine Majesty. So he is now as far above the angels as the title which he has inherited is higher than their own name (Heb 1:1-4)*

If the glory of God's divinity shines now through the frailty and lowliness of His humanity, when He came to earth He — who was one with God — didn't deem it an honor to hold on to but He emptied Himself, taking upon Himself the form of a servant. And being even more humble, He was obedient unto death, the death of the cross (Ph 2:6-8). St. Luke tells us that Jesus was subject to human laws of growth just as we are: "And Jesus increased in wisdom, in nature, and in favor with God and men" (Lk 2:52).

He spent, as tradition holds, about thirty three years on this earth, radiating in His teachings, healings and miracles the infinite love of the heavenly Father toward His children. Almost thirty of those years were spent in hidden silence in a small, out-of-the-way village of Nazareth. And so, from His silent birth in Bethlehem until His death on Calvary, Jesus was wrapt in the silence of God. And in this He taught us in what true human greatness consists.

To Do The Will Of The Father

HIS EARTHLY LIFE was an arduous pilgrimage to the Father carried out in silence, worship and surrendering love. Tempted as we are in all things, He never sinned (Heb 4:15). Nonetheless, His journey to the right hand of the Father where He reigns today in glory was a constant struggle with His human desires in order to bring them into perfect conformity to the Father's will, the one thing which He had come to do: "To do your will, O God, is my delight" (Ps 40:9).

In a series of "not I" statements, Jesus asserts His role as a humble servant of His Father from His earliest, conscious moments of human existence:

> *The Son can do nothing by himself;*
> *He can do only what he sees the Father doing:*
> *and whatever the Father does, the Son does too (Jn 5:19)*
>
> *I can do nothing by myself;*
> *I can only judge as I am told to judge. . . (Jn 5:30).*
>
> *. . . because I have come from heaven,*
> *not to do my own will,*
> *but to do the will of the one who sent me (Jn 7:16).*
>
> *And my word is not my own:*
> *it is the word of the one who sent me (Jn 14:24).*

In these statements, Jesus reveals an inner consciousness of His ultimate worth and meaning as a human being that derives from His complete dependence on the Father. He seeks only to please His Father. This was what was behind His thirty years of silence at Nazareth. He was like us in every way. He had a human body with its physical, psychic and spiritual powers. As he labored in the carpenter shop at

Nazareth, He felt fatigue, hunger and thirst. His sexual powers developed and matured normally during His adolescent years at Nazareth. And His greatest struggle during those years was to integrate all the riches of His person in such a way that His humanity would reflect as perfectly as possible its oneness with His divinity.

He had to learn by experience how best to offer His body and mind and all their powers in submissive love to His indwelling divinity. He grew everyday through prayer and docility to the Father. He became adept at silencing His inner clamorings to do what He wanted in order to find the greatest freedom in surrendering His whole being to glorify the Father. The monotonous work He performed — hardly creative in the worldly sense — had its own role to play. "He who sent me is with me and has not left me to myself, for I always do what pleases him" (Jn 8:29).

In Silent Self-Surrender

As JESUS grew daily, He learned to turn more inwardly to find His Father at the center of His being (Jn 14:11). There in the depths of His heart, He, who was the one "closest to the heart of His Father" (Jn 1:18), breathed, smiled, laughed and cried in that holy presence. Gerard Manley Hopkins, S.J., writes in a short poem what I conceive must have been the habitual framework of reference in which Jesus was constantly the Gift to the Father, the Giver of all good things:

> *Thee God I come from,*
> *To Thee go.*
> *All day long I like fountain flow,*
> *From Thy hand out,*
> *Swayed about*
> *Mote-like*
> *In Thy mighty glow.*

In a daily rhythm of prayer, hard work, obedience to His mother Mary, to Joseph and His fellow townspeople, Jesus strove for that inner peace which He in His public preaching would refer to as "poverty of spirit" (Mt 5:3). He recognized it as the basis for entering into the Kingdom of heaven. Whether He sat on a hillside above Nazareth looking into the smiling face of His Father reflected in the fluffy white clouds or whether He was alone doing rough carpentry, He was inwardly silent and turned toward the Father as the Center of His life. He learned to close the door of His inner closet (Mt 6:6) and there in silence and truth adore His Father.

Gentleness characterized Jesus' every gesture, word and deed. He lovingly handled the wood He worked with in the carpenter shop. He took delight in the fiery sunset which spangled the West with flaming colors. He found joy in sheep, in vineyards, in the bread He ate at table. All inspired thoughts of praise and thanksgiving as He silently offered the sentiments of His heart to the Father in love and adoration. Nothing could take Him from the love of His Father. Inwardly He was bathed in silent communication with Him Who was the Source of His being. Prayer was as natural to Him as breathing.

We marvel that, after thirty years of such inner silence and external retirement from the hustle and bustle of the world and its big cities crowded with people, Jesus was not only ready but eager to leave Nazareth to begin His journey to the heart of Jerusalem where He would enter into His deepest and final hour of silence.

The Public Life Of Christ

JESUS BEGAN His public work of announcing the inbreaking of the Kingdom of heaven in His person by lining up with sinners to be baptized by John in the Jordan. He who was sinless made Himself to be reckoned among sinners, so great was his burning zeal to become one with us in all things. When He emerged from the water, He could hear His Father's voice from heaven declare: "This is my Son, the Beloved; my favor rests on him" (Mt 3:17).

Jesus pleased the Father because He was His "spitting image." He had come, not to be served, but to serve. And His ultimate service would be to surrender His life for all of us to ransom us back from the kingdom of sin and death (Mt 20:29; Mk 10:45). He was, as John the Baptist declared, the Lamb of God who takes away the sin of the world (Jn 1:29). He would perfectly fulfill, by His silent suffering on our behalf, the prophecy of the Suffering Servant as foretold by Isaiah the prophet:

> *Harshly dealt with, he bore it humbly,*
> *he never opened his mouth,*
> *like a lamb that is led to the slaughter-house,*
> *like a sheep that is dumb before its shearers*
> *never opening its mouth (Is 53:7).*

Temptations In The Desert

JESUS WAS LED by the Spirit into the silence of the desert (Mk 1:12), and there He was tempted. These forty days and forty nights were merely symbolic of the kind of temptations that would confront Him all His life. Jesus remained sinless and holy because He yielded to God's Spirit within Him and rejected the clamorous promptings of the devil urging Him to declare His independence from the Father. We see from the Synoptic accounts of Jesus' temptations in the desert how the early Christians testified to their belief that Jesus progressed in holiness by overcoming these temptations (see Mt 4:1-11; Mk 1:13; Lk 4:1-13). The basic truth that comes to us from reading these Gospel accounts of Christ's temptation is that He had to struggle mightily within His heart to reach that state of inner equilibrium, peace and integration which would climax in the silent expiration of His final breath on the cross as he humbly submitted for the last time to the Father's holy will.

The holiness of the Lord is seen, not only as the presence of the Father's Spirit in Him giving Him strength to unmask and defeat the devil or the principle of darkness, but also as the end product of a growth process in which Jesus necessarily had to confront the Evil One and conquer him. The three temptations highlight Jesus' total attachment to His Father. Even the suggestion of doing anything which would separate Him from that love is abhorrent to Him. In all of the temptation accounts of the New Testament, He is presented as the counterpart to Eve — the symbol of the *anima* in us all — and her struggle against temptation in the garden of Eden. Where she failed, He went on to succeed.

The basic temptation in His life was to speak His own words rather than to be the Father's Word to the world, to take the initiative into His own hands rather than wait upon the Father, to assert His own rather than the Father's sovereignty. He rejected all three. "Man does not live by bread alone but by every word which comes from the mouth of God." He would not yield to feed Himself on anything but God's word. "You must worship the Lord your God and serve Him alone" (Dt 6:13; Lk 4:8). Power and glory were rejected by Him in deference to the sovereignty of God. Finally, He claims His divine origin, not by presuming on His divine power to protect Him, but on an inner poverty of spirit reflected in His absolute dependence upon the Father's goodness: "You must not put the Lord your God to the test" (Lk 4:12).

The physical desert, a symbol of the inner desert within all of us, including Jesus, has a power to reduce us to basics. Jesus had to struggle all His earthly existence to be His true self, the Image of the heavenly Father, the silent Word through which the Mind of God would speak of unselfish love to the world. Jesus grew through each event and circumstance of each day as He sought to image the Father's holiness by doing, not His own but the Father's will: "Here I am! I am coming to obey Your will" (Heb 10:9).

Silent Gentleness

FROM THE PAGES of the Gospels we see how Jesus moved about doing good wherever He went, actively ministering to others by preaching God's Word of love and bringing healing and hope to the oppressed and the maimed. In the midst of a veritable plethora of activities, fatiguing journeys on foot, attacks by the opposing religious leaders of His day and even rejection by those whom He had lovingly served, Jesus shows us a consistent picture of one integrated on body, soul and spirit levels.

His invitation to all was — and is: "Come to me, all you who labor and are overburdened, and I will give you rest. Shoulder my yoke and learn from me, for I am gentle and humble in heart, and you will find rest for your souls. Yes, my yoke is easy and my burden light" (Mt 11:28-30). To everyone He met He showed a gentleness that He had learned from His heavenly Father. Gentleness in God and in Christ is not weakness. It is strength to give one's life in love for others. It is to attain an inner peace and quiet that we allow Jesus to take our lives (in the language of love) and to silently offer them as a sacrifice that any person who comes to claim such a love from us may find the happiness they seek.

Jesus experienced and testified to the reality that the Father always was working and He, too, in gentleness worked with Him (Jn 5:17). This freed Him to become totally human, to be totally alive in every moment, to the Father's infinite love, inbreaking in the context of the human situation. It was His constant, silent standing in the loving presence of His Father that allowed Him to be gentle and docile to the Father's Spirit, working within His heart.

The Birds Of The Air And The Lilies Of The Field

IN HIS many references to nature, to the inanimate, as well as to the plant and animal worlds around Him, Jesus reveals to us His sensitivity, His gentle receptivity toward the material world, permeated as it is by His Father's uncreated energies of love. Lambs freshly born, seeds sown in the soft earth, the rain with its cleansing power, the birds that never stored grain into barns, the fox in its den, the grape vines being pruned, the flaming sunset, all creatures proclaimed to the gentle Lord that His Father was near, holy and good, beautiful and loving. Jesus, too, wanted to be beautiful and gentle, loving and true in His silent, adoring surrender to the Father.

> Think of the ravens. They do not sow or reap; they have no storehouses and no barns; yet God feeds them. And how much more are you worth than the birds!. . . Think of the flowers; they never have to spin or weave; yet I assure you, not even Solomon in all his regalia was robed like one of these. Now if that is how God clothes the grass in the field which is there today and thrown into the furnace tomorrow, how much more will he look after you, you men of little faith!. . . Your Father well knows you need them. No; set your hearts on his kingdom, and these other things will be given you

*as well. There is no need to be afraid, little flock, for it has pleased
your Father to give you the kingdom (Lk 12:24-32).*

God's Presence In People

IF JESUS, in silence, could perceive the voice of His Father's
creative love in each plant and animal, how much more in
greater silence would He hear the Word of the Father's love
speak to Him in the gifts of human beings who came into
His life? Perhaps He most keenly sensed His Father's presence in the intimate communion that He had with His
mother, Mary, and with Joseph, His foster-father. Surely
Mary had a tremendous influence in shaping His attitudes
and molding His character. If lovers can communicate with
each other in ever deepening silence as their love grows in
purity, she and Jesus must have been able to communicate
to one another — in deepest silence — the love of God that
was poured out into both of their hearts for each other.

Every person who ever encountered the Lord was, for
Him, an incarnation of the Father's unique love for that
person. In silencing His own heart, Jesus came into contact
with the silent love of the Father in the other and responded
in kind. "As the Father has loved me, so I have loved you"
(Jn 15:9). He loved Lazarus and wept over him in the tomb.
He loved Mary and Martha and stayed as a guest in their
home. How sensitively He listened to the godly in each of
His disciples. He loved Peter differently from John; James
differently from Judas. By word and example, look and
touch, He shared Himself most intimately with the twelve
who accompanied Him for three years, day and night. He
shared Himself with them in the even deeper intimacy of
silence. With tender love He washed their feet (Jn 13:4-11).
He gave His own body and blood that they, eating and
drinking, might share His own divine life forever. He

breathed upon them after His resurrection and gave them
His Spirit. Then He commissioned them to forgive sins and
heal the sick as He did (Mk 16:16-20).

He reprimanded these same disiciples when they sought
to turn away the little children who only wanted to touch
Him. "Let the little children come to me; do not stop them;
for it is to such as these that the kingdom of God belongs"
(Mk 10:14). With what inner silence and gentle love did He
minister to the sick, the possessed, the sinful who came to
Him in droves, never to be turned away for He had come as
a Shepherd to bring the lost sheep back to the Father's fold.

Some modern psychologists have sought to determine
from the Gospel stories of Christ during His public ministry
what personality "type" He was. What we find in the pages
of the Gospels is a person, integrated and loving at all times.
He is introvert and extrovert, rational and intuitive, feeling
and sensate. He has a highly developed *animus* (focused
consciousness) as well as a highly developed *anima* (diffused
awareness). He was a man for all seasons, one who strove to
be all things to all persons. He, who was the image of the
heavenly Father, remained silently at the center of His being
in the deepest possible oneness with His loving Father. He
allowed His Holy Spirit to permeate His entire being — His
finger tips, His eyes, His hearing, His voice, His gestures —
in order to give full expression to His love and the love of the
Father towards each and every individual who approached
Him with openness and faith.

A Just Anger

YET THIS GENTLE, loving Jesus could show anger in an
admonishing way to those who lived lives of pride and
deceit. In His judgments, He was capable of giving vent to
the "wrath of God" who gave Him the right to judge (Jn

5:22). The Father "appointed him supreme judge" (Jn 5:27). And so we also see in the Gospel accounts how Jesus slashed out at the hypocrisy of the Pharisees and Scribes (Lk 11:37-40; Jn 5:37; Mt 12:24-25, 31-34).

His strong indictment of false religious leaders, who imposed on the people such burdens as they themselves did not observe, came out of an inner silence that allowed Him to hear the Father speak to Him as how best to respond in love to those not living in love. In Chapter 23 of St. Matthew's Gospel we find these angry words on the lips of Jesus: "Hypocrites!," "Whitewashed tombs!," "Serpents, brood of vipers!" But they are spoken without disturbing His inner peace for they flowed from that inner silence which was able to cover each accusing word with the correcting love of the Father.

Zeal for His Father's house — which the merchants and money changers had turned into a market place (Mt 21:12-13) — motivated Jesus to drive them physically from the temple precincts without ever losing His inner calm. During His passion and especially at the time of His suffering on the cross, Jesus offered a prayer of loving forgiveness to His Father on behalf of His offenders: "Father, forgive them; they do not know what they are doing" (Lk 23:34).

Jesus's silence did not make Him weak in any sense of the word. He turned upon Peter and rebuked him angrily because Peter had his own ideas of how Jesus should restore the kingdom of Israel and his ideas had nothing to do with suffering and death. "Get behind me, Satan! You are an obstacle in my path, because the way you think is not God's way but man's" (Mt 16:23). He lovingly forgave Peter when Peter betrayed Him. Indeed, in all of His human relationships, Jesus strove to act and reach from out of the silent core of His being where He was centered completely upon the Father's will and not upon His own way of thinking.

Love Is Silent Surrender

NOWHERE DO WE SEE the struggle between Jesus' own will and that of His heavenly Father as clearly as in His agony in the Garden of Gethsemane. Here is a picture of a person confronting the areas of His being that would wish to have His own words, His own plans done. Jesus truly did not want to die. He prayed to the heavenly Father that if there would be any way whereby He could please Him and still live, He would want that to be done. But, if it were the Father's will that Jesus should die for the salvation of the world, then He was ready. No self-centered cries from within Jesus could drown out the silent surrender of His will to do what most pleased the Father. "Father, if you are willing, take this cup away from me. Nevertheless, let your will be done, not mine" (Lk 22:42).

On the cross after hours of excruciating pain, Jesus offered up His life like a silent Lamb brought to the slaughter (Is 53:7). Becoming like "water draining away" (Is 22:14), Jesus entered into the darkness of abandonment that came over His human consciousness. Earlier He had bathed His consciousness in the warm light of the Father's loving face and found the strength to do whatever most pleased Him. Now that loving face seemed to disappear, leaving Him alone in a stark and deathly darkness. He sank deeper and deeper into that darkness, through spaces in His hitherto unexplored sub-conscious mind. He fell into a deep and silent void where He confronted His last and greatest temptation.

Earth, sky and air suddenly froze and became still before the awesome white figure hanging on the cross. The cry of Jesus pierced the darkened silence:

My God, my God, why have you deserted me?
How far from saving me, the words I groan!
I call all day, my God, but you never answer,
all night long I call and cannot rest (Ps 22:1-2).

Fear, doubt, rejection flooded over Jesus as the clamor of the crowd threatened to disrupt the habitual silence that reigned in His heart all His human life. Had He been deluded in thinking He was one with the Father? Were His miracles and healings truly of the Father or were they from some kind of demonic angel of light? Jesus, the Warrior Lord, dismissed these unruly intruders into His peace, and strained to catch a glimpse of the Father's reassuring face. "When the sixth hour came, there was darkness over the whole land until the ninth hour. And at the ninth hour Jesus cried out in a loud voice, 'Eloi, Eloi, lama sabachthani?' which means, 'My God, my God, why have you deserted me?' " (Mk 15:33-34).

In such ultimate brokenness of body, soul and spirit, Jesus became humanly conscious of the self-emptying love that had always been His from all eternity. He was being asked, in the supreme language of human love, to lay down His life for His friends. Surrendering lovingly to the Father's will, He said, "It is accomplished." Then bowing His head, He died (Jn 19:30). As the soft, velvety fingers of dawn gently lift the veil of darkness from the face of the earth to let the sun burst upon the horizon with full radiance, so in deepest silence within the heart of Christ the light of the Father's love softly fell upon His broken spirit and drove away the darkness of despair and the noises of doubt. The Father had "not hidden his face from him but has answered him when he called" (Ps 22:24).

Listen To The Word In Silence

IN HIS DEATH, Jesus passed over to a new life of glory. In His resurrectional presence through His Spirit, He can now abide in us, members of His body, the Church. He, who in His humanity silently listened to God as He spoke His Word in Him, now speaks in deepest silence from the depths of His disciples' hearts. If we listen and obey His Word, He promises that He and the Father will make their home in us. "If anyone loves me he will keep my word, and my father will love him, and we shall come to him and make our home with him" (Jn 14:23).

Jesus works silently and gently in our heart if we have learned to be silent listeners to His Word. He is silently present and powerfully works for us in His sacraments. He speaks quietly in the Church's preaching and teaching of His Word. He is silent, like leaven inserted into a mass of dough, as He seeks to reconcile the world (Col 1:20) to His Father.

He is most powerfully present in us as the silent Word of God when we, like St. Stephen and the numerous martyrs down to our present age, suffer with Him and for Him in loving, surrendering silence. For then we know — as St. Ignatius of Antioch, who was martyred in Rome (105 A.D.) as witness to Christ as God's silent Word, came to know — that we are Christians. To suffer joyfully for the Lord is an unmistakable sign that the Spirit of love has driven out our noisy, self-centered words and has replaced them with the one, silent Word of God, who is Jesus, the Messiah.

CHAPTER SIX

Woman Wrapt In Silence

As STAR DIFFERS from star, so there are many different kinds of silence. There is the silence of the forest when no leaf is stirring. There is the eerie silence on the battlefield as enemies hold their fire before the kill. Two lovers reach a union of love that silences all words. And then, there is the silence of death.

Perhaps God's silence, even the silence of His incarnate Word, Jesus Christ, is too much for us mortals to understand. We have ears to hear but we fail to hear the intense silence of the indwelling Trinity. God, in His loving providence, gives us Mary as an archetype of what we are all called to become. We can hear her silence better than that of God. We can gaze at the Moon with ease, but find it difficult to gaze directly into the face of the Sun.

Mary refracts for us in human experiences the holiness of God. She holds out to us in terms of human growth what we human beings, by God's grace, can hope to become. She stands before us as the first Christian, the first human being to become totally conscious that Jesus Christ lives in her, and she surrenders totally in faith and loving obedience to serve Him. As a pilgrim from the beginning of her life to the end on this earth, she progresses further and further in her appreciation of God as the Source of her entire being. She lives in "connected aloneness" with the Alone and thus becomes a bridge bringing all other creatures into the loving worship of God. She is also the first-born of the Church — which is an individual or a collectivity of individuals in whom Christ's Spirit dwells and operates to produce His fruit of love, peace and joy, the signs of His presence in the world. She is in a miniature form what the whole Church is destined to become by God's divinizing grace.

What she has been called to and has attained by God's grace, God also calls us to every moment to attain by the help of His constant grace. Karl Rahner makes this important point:

> *God has eternally kept His eternal love in readiness for us too, so that in the moment that we call our baptism, He may come into the depths of our heart. For we too are redeemed, saved, marked with God's indelible seal. We too have been made the holy temple of God. In us too the triune God dwells. We too have been sent by Him, from this beginning, into our life, that we too may carry the light of faith and the flame of love through this world's darkness, to the place we belong in His eternal radiance, His eternity* (Mary Mother of the Lord, *p. 49*).

On A Journey

WE HAVE PERHAPS for too long conceived Mary's holiness in static terms. This has made her "abnormally" holy, in a way that we could never imitate or attain. Vatican Council II well describes Mary as a *viator*, a pilgrim on a journey. Her growth in God's divine life unfolded in her as she cooperated with His grace and exercised faith, hope and love in the context of her concrete human situation.

She, like us, was in need of the redeeming grace of the only Mediator, Jesus Christ. ". . . because she belongs to the offspring of Adam, she is one with all human beings in their need for salvation" (*Constitution on the Church*, #52). "She stands out among the poor and humble of the Lord who confidently hope for and receive salvation from him" (*Ibid.*, #55). She had to discover in each moment of her life God's love and surrender to do His holy will. She had to push her consciousness, always by the power of the Holy Spirit, to new levels of awareness that God was All, the Source, in whom she in her emptiness found her fullness.

In her poverty and humility, Mary gradually grew in a surrendering adoration that was actualized by her fidelity to do at all times God's holy will in her regard. Her holiness or human integration of all gifts of creation into a wholeness unfolded in the context of her daily life as she silently listened to God's Word and pondered it in her heart. She *grew* into ever fuller degrees of grace by yielding herself to the promptings of God's Spirit. Like us, she too had to cooperate with God's grace at each moment of her life.

God As Mother

HUMAN BEINGS are totally sexual beings. Our sexuality is locked up inside each and every atom of our being. It exerts a unique response to God's daily call to enter into more intimate union with Him and with all His creatures, especially all human creatures who come into our lives.

Mary was the perfect woman, truly created in the image and likeness of God. "Male and female He created them" (Gn 1:27). If her femininity in some way images God, is it unthinkable that, in her very physical sexuality as virgin and mother, Mary experienced God as Woman, God as Mother?

God's invitation to her at the annunciation, His word to

her during the time of her expectation, was that she be as fully feminine, as fully virginal and as truly maternal as God is. In surrendering herself to God's will, she experienced, not only a new sense of herself as a woman, loved infinitely by God, but she also experienced God in an entirely new way, a way that was at once feminine and maternal.

She expereinced God bringing forth a Son through the Spirit. She experienced the fact that together they were giving birth to Him. In mystical ecstasy she experienced the growth of the child within her from conception to birth as she grew from virgin to mother, from a state of receptivity to an ever greater fullness of grace without losing either.

She experienced the Spirit giving birth within *her* to something unique, re-creating *her* as a new person in God, enabling *her* to be spiritually born again and again on ever newer, higher levels of grace. She was filled with an inner joy that can only be described by the word, *contentment*. Contentment is the state of being satisfied, fulfilled, at peace. It describes a child at its mother's breast, fully present to itself in the moment, yet fully caught up in a kind of ecstatic oneness with its mother. The past and the future are embraced in the present, nourishing moment. There is no fear. Like a child full of wonder, Mary knew that oneness with God, the Source of her life, the Be-All and End-All of her existence. Her contentment in the Spirit describes her sense of being at home in God's protective love, surrounded by God's maternal care and concern. All external and internal turmoil were dispelled by God's all important presence.

Living In The Present Moment

FROM EARLY CHILDHOOD, Mary experienced God as ever guiding her, protecting her as any loving Mother would her child. She learned to penetrate the ordinariness of each moment and to discover God inside the materiality of it. She quickly came to see the "connectedness" between every creature she encountered and the God who brought that creature into existence, Who was the Giver of Life, the One in whom we all live and move and have our being (Ac 17:28).

"Commit your fate to Yahweh, trust in Him and He will act" (Ps 37:3-5) became a way of life to her. Filled with childlike trust, she found it easy to abandon herself with joy and peace to whatever might be God's will. Daily she gave thanks to God, her Mother/Father (1 Th 5:18) for all things "bright and beautiful" which she accepted as gifts to her from on high. Because she found her strength completely in God, the Source of all power, she was the happiest of all human beings. In her poverty, she felt God's providence sustaining her as a weak eaglet finds confidence to fly when supported by the mother eagle's wings (Dt 32:11).

If Jesus could relate to God as masculine ("My Father goes on working, and so do I," Jn 5:18), Mary could relate to God as feminine, and this developed in her a profound hope. Hope was begotten in her as she confessed her own weakness. It enabled her to trust in God's goodness and holiness. And it produced a reverence in her that made it possible for her to surrender totally to God's unfolding will.

> *My soul proclaims the greatness of the Lord*
> *and my spirit exults in God my saviour;*
> *because he has looked upon his lowly handmaid.*
> *Yes, from this day forward all generations will call me blessed,*
> *for the Almighty has done great things for me.*
> *Holy is his name. . . (Lk 1:46-49).*

She silenced the nagging voice in her heart that sought to persuade her to take control of her own life and to shape future events. How balanced she was, swinging from the *now* to embrace the Eternal: "I am the handmaid of the Lord; let what you have said be done to me" (Lk 1:38). It is the feminine element in her — and in all of us — that is the unifying force in human living because it does not fear to surrender to Love. Mary lived deeply in the silence of the present moment. And it was there that she found God's will speaking to her softly in His indwelling Word. But most of us are not dwellers in the present moment. We strain to embrace the future as *we* envision it, often to our own undoing. We drown out God's Word as we fill our hearts with the noisy clamor of our own designs for tomorrow, whereas our "future" depends on our humbly hearing and obeying His Word in the grace of the present moment.

Leonardo da Vinci, with great precision, describes the inner pull between God drawing us ever more intimately into His life and our own anxiety about the future as we would wish it to be:

> *Everything, everyone, wants to go back to the original chaos, like the butterfly that insists on being burned in the candle flame. Man is always longing for next spring, next summer, future months, new years. It always seems to him that the thing he lusts after never comes soon enough. Yet he never realizes that all he is asking for, in fact, is his own destruction, his own unmaking. And this desire, so unconscious and deep within him, is of his very essence. He has the spirit in him and this spirit, being aware that it is shut up in a human body, is always longing to get back to the one who put it there.*

Mary, seeking the face of God in each event, was able to discover a new incarnation in each present moment. We could say that God is again taking on "flesh," breaking into her world to pitch His tent near her, to bring His *shekinah* of infinite glory into the darkened world around her. Mary

teaches us in her inner integration and "connected aloneness" that only in the present moment does God meet us and
bring us into new life in His Word. With wonder — as Mary
lived — we too can embrace the presence of God in each
event and enter with her into the great adventure called life.
We are invited, as she was, to share in God's creative, loving
energies. We are called to co-create with Him — out of the
raw stuff of each moment — the only real world there is,
namely the world of living and loving in God's holy will.

Inner Silence Illumined By Faith

To ATTAIN that "still point" in any given point of time, we
need to open ourselves to God's gift to us of the present
moment. By faith we "see" God, get in touch with His loving
activities and then work with Him to effect a transformation
to something better. Because of her humility and faith,
Mary brought forth from her own body and blood the body
and blood of God's only begotten Son. Her milk became His
food. In the course of her life she changed wool into cloth,
wheat into bread, suffering into joy and resurrection. The
faith which gave her inner peace and silence illumines us in a
freeing way, enabling us see God inside of each moment.
But there is also a freeing — by faith — from ourselves and
from the limitations that we place upon ourselves and others
in any given situation. We learn to believe — as Mary always
did — that what is impossible to us is possible to God
(Lk 1:37). The negativity of holding that we and others can
only do so much is transcended by faith which enables us to
proclaim to ourselves and to the world: "I can do all things in
Him who strengthened me" (Ph 4:13).

True faith does not lead to presumption, but to a true
assessment of each situation. It enables us to prudently
discern what we can do with God's help to change matters

according to His holy will. True gentleness and meekness are rooted in humility, making it possible for us to view reality through the eyes of faith and from God's perspective. Faith in God's infinite love is rooted in the Word of God. Faith teaches us, through the illumination of the Holy Spirit, to have, as Mary did, an uncompromising openness to God's call in the history of salvation. "He has come to the help of Israel his servant, mindful of his mercy to Abraham and to his descendants for ever" (Lk 1:54-55).

Connected Aloneness

AGAINST THE BACKDROP of a western world ruled by such symbols of masculine power as science, technology, agressiveness and rugged individualism, Mary stands as the symbol of the eternal feminine. She cries out to all of us in her strong but delicate, tender but enduring obedience to God's holy will that we become truly human first by becoming truly feminine, diffusedly aware of God's loving presence within and around us. Only when we realize the Mary in us — the feminine openness to God's free gift of Himself to us in our lives— will we begin to be what God has destined us to become. The feminine in us, as in Mary, develops within us gradually and leads us to fully integrated personalities only when we learn to let go of the conscious control we hold over our lives and surrender them in inner poverty to God's gift of grace.

Mary knew how to concentrate. She was a truly centered person. In her concentration, she progressively found God to be her Center and Source, the One from whom she received her name and personhood. She lived in the "heart of her heart," that inner enclosed garden where she mystically surrendered in love to the Bridegroom of her soul.

> *She is a garden enclosed,*
> *my sister, my promised bride;*
> *a garden enclosed, a sealed fountain (Sg 4:12).*

In that Spirit-filled garden she knew her God and her knowledge united her to Him in the experience of a loving union. And God's love, which overshadowed her in the silent, humble self-surrender of her being, bore the fruit of Love. St. John of the Cross' beautiful words apply to Mary:

> *She lived in solitude,*
> *And now in solitude has built her nest;*
> *And in solitude He guides her,*
> *He alone, Who also bears*
> *in solitude the wound of love* (Spiritual Canticle, *Stanza 35*).

Growth In Freedom

IT WAS Mary's silence which allowed her to live in such a profound openness to God's Word of love. It was her silence which freed her to romp with Him playfully on the mountain-tops of ecstatic union. Because of her silence, she could truly make the words of Habakkuk the prophet her own: "Yahweh my Lord is my strength, he makes my feet as light as a doe's, he sets my steps on the heights" (Hab 3:19).

But to attain such inner silence, Mary had to consciously strive to be attentive to the Word of God that she pondered so faithfully in her heart (Lk 2:20, 52). She experienced, through her silence and loving surrender to that Word, what Jesus himself had promised: "If you make my word your home you will indeed be my disciples; you will learn the truth and the truth will make you free" (Jn 8:31-32).

Mary is our model of true human freedom. This does not consist primarily in being free to choose between good and evil. This is the lowest kind of freedom that we human beings experience. There is another freedom to which God calls us through inner silence and surrendering love. This freedom, which Mary progressively attained, gives one the ability to know, through the Holy Spirit, the *indicative* state of dignity that God's free grace has bestowed on us. This maturity in the spiritual life comes before we respond to God's call to keep His Word. Then in the light of our inner dignity, we are able to take our lives into our own hands and return them totally to God, love for Love. The *imperative* which follows upon this realization and of which St. Paul so often speaks is the peak of human freedom. Mary was perfectly free to love God — not through fear, restraint or an imperative of duty or command of law. With her whole being, she recognized that she could not live without the Lord. She freely determined to live her life at every moment according to the will of God, and in so doing she knew that she was the freest of all human beings. Living consciously in God, with God and for God, through total virginal surrender, brought her at each step of the way to a greater freedom, a greater desire and ability to allow God to be supreme in her life.

This does not mean that silence is freedom. Silence is the preparation, the environment in which one can surrender to God's Word and become free in loving submission to His will. Progressive appreciation and actual living in silence of body, soul and spirit relationships brings with them a progressive awakening and awareness of the perfect love of God. Deeper serenity, peace, joy and stability of life result as the fruits of the working of the Holy Spirit within (Gal 5:22).

The Strength Of Silence

THERE IS nothing weak about silence. It centers us and gives us great inner power. In the life of Mary we see that, like Jesus, she too was tempted both from within and from without. She needed in faith, hope and love to turn in silence to the inner Source of all strength. She had to struggle, as we do, with the ambiguities of her daily human situation, and bring them under God's tutelage and wisdom in child-like abandonment. She worried and suffered: ". . . and his mother said to him, 'My child, why have you done this to us? See how worried your father and I have been, looking for you.' 'Why were you looking for me?' he replied. 'Did you not know that I must be busy with my Father's affairs?' But they did not understand what he meant" (Lk 2:48-50).

What temptations to despair must have assailed her as she stood silently at the foot of the cross before her dying Son! In that hour of utter darkness, Mary's motherly heart was torn in two at the terrifying sight of her Son's agonizing death. With Him, she passes from the holding on to life to a complete giving up of life. With Him she suffers the extreme physical pain and spiritual anguish of dying. She experiences in the very core of her being the truth of the prophecy of Isaiah: "The heart of each man fails him, they are terrified, pangs and pains seize them, they writhe like a woman in labor" (Is 13:7-8). She is asked to relinquish possession of her own life and to let go of the only thing in her life that even mattered, holding on to Jesus as *her* Son. The "fiat," which she had pronounced at the annunciation and countless times thereafter throughout her life, reached its full realization at the foot of the cross. Silence had prepared her for a theophany of God's love in the symbol of a pierced heart, from which poured forth blood and water to the very last drop.

Love For Others

FROM THE INNER DEPTHS of her consciousness, centered on the indwelling Trinity within her, peace and harmony flowed outward to bring to her body and all its movements a radiant peace. Her touch, speech, walking or sitting, everything about her breathed an inner harmony that was expressed exteriorly to all who met her. If mothers exert a tremendous influence, far greater as a rule than fathers, in shaping the attitude and character of their children, it is only reasonable to believe that Jesus learned most of His gentle traits and loving ways as well as the harmonious carriage of the precious treasure of God's divinity within Him, from His mother, Mary.

A wise person is known not only by fewness of words, but by the power of God's Word which is released in each significant syllable uttered. When Mary spoke in the humble home where she lived with her husband, Joseph, the carpenter, and with Jesus, how empowered must have been the words she spoke! Kneading bread in her kitchen, cleaning the floors, fetching water from the village well, making up the beds, Mary was a woman truly wrapt in silence. Her centering upon God gave her a God-like insight into everything. God shone diaphanously through all the material creatures that she touched with loving care. The poetic words of William Blake well describe Mary in her silent adoration of God in all of His creation:

> To see the World in a Grain of Sand
> And Heaven in a Wild Flower,
> Hold Infinity in the palm of your hand
> And Eternity in an hour (Auguries of Innocence).

Love of God — begotten in silence — also begets the love of other human beings. As Mary experienced in prayer

God's love calling her to participate in a return of love, she became progressively freer to love others by seeking to serve them. Touching the Center of the wheel of life, Mary touched in loving oneness all the spokes that moved, knowingly or unknowingly, to that same Center. She knew the paradox that to be free is to become a slave to serve others in love. She knew that she was called to this service of others in love and this was her greatest privilege.

We see her gentle concern for others at the wedding feast of Cana. Such sensitivity to the needs of the guests came from her total silence on other occasions. She anticipated the embarrassment of the newlyweds by informing her Son, ever so tactfully: "They have no wine" (Jn 2:3). Sensitive, totally feminine, Mary was open to the needs of all. Jesus learned from His mother how to be silent, gentle, compassionate and loving, toward all.

T.S. Eliot well expresses the paradox of Mary's silence that gives her the power to speak, of her emptying that God can fill her with the Kingdom of Heaven, to care and not to care, to be, in a word, authentically what God's holy will silently speaks her to be when He speaks her name in His Word.

> *Blessed sister, holy mother, spirit of the fountain,*
>   *spirit of the garden,*
> *Suffer us not to mock ourselves with falsehood*
> *Teach us to care and not to care*
> *Teach us to be still*
> *even among these rocks.*
> *Our peace in his will*
> *And even among these rocks*
> *Sister, mother,*
> *And spirit of the river, spirit of the sea.*
> *Suffer me not to be separated*
> *And let my cry come unto Thee* (Ash Wednesday).

CHAPTER SEVEN

Silence In Human Love

WE RECEIVE our existence in and through a human community, the family. It is in a loving community that we best evolve the potential within us to become fully human by discovering our unique identity in a loving I-Thou relationship.

The kind of isolation that breeds loneliness not only destroys such a loving community but brings destruction to our entire being as well. How strong the effects of such isolated loneliness are was graphically demonstrated by the French scientist, Dr. Michel Siffre. As part of a scientific experiment, he remained alone in an underground room for 205 days. This was 100 feet below ground, in Midnight Cave, near Del Rio, Texas.

He had all the food he needed, reading and recreational material and a certain number of scientific tests to carry out each day. For the first third of the time the scientist maintained good physical health and remained well adjusted both mentally and physically. After the second month, however, he began to feel almost suffocated by the loneliness. He started to show signs of physical, mental and emotional deterioration. On the 86th day he contemplated committing suicide. A week later he was still hanging on, but wrote: "I am living through the nadir of my life. This long loneliness is beyond all bearing."

Solitude and aloneness were bringing him into a deeper awareness of himself. "When you find yourself alone," he wrote, "isolated in a world totally without time, face to face with yourself, all the masks that you hid behind — those to preserve your own illusions, those that project them before others — finally fall, sometimes brutally." A touching relief came into his drab existence when a field mouse found its way into Midnight Cave. Siffre plotted how he would capture it and thus have a "living friend" to dispel his sense of loneliness somewhat. He tried to put a casserole dish over the poor creature to capture it but in the attempt he struck the mouse and killed it. "He is still," he wrote. "Desolation overwhelms me."

We will do just about anything to make contact with another living being, especially another living human being, in order to establish a sharing community. This burning need to communicate with others is the way God made us, so that through communication with others we might reach some level of communion in love. We have been made by God out of His infinite love to give love and to receive it in return. When this becomes impossible, we become dehumanized.

Begetting Of The I

GABRIEL MARCEL, the noted French Catholic philosopher, succinctly expressed this need when he wrote: "The *I* is the child of the *We*." In our human frailty we human beings seek to establish a community of loving, caring persons where we can find healing from our loneliness and re-birth through their love. When we are first born, we live a very primitive sort of existence, following instincts which are basically "self-serving." As we develop — through discipline, education and experience — we discover ourselves to be subjects, individuals, persons. The world of objects is "over there" while we are "over here." We maintain certain distinctions between ourselves and them by our ability to put other persons and things into rational and impersonal "boxes."

But to all of us there comes the call of God's Spirit of love inviting us to enter into a higher level of existence where we experience a higher degree of human consciousness and come to recognize the uniqueness of our own and other's being. At the heart of God is the loving community of the Trinity. God is love (1 Jn 4:8). Love is a call to enter fully into oneself through an intimate surrendering of that self to another. In the ecstasy of "standing outside" of themselves and becoming available through the gift of love to live for one another, the Persons of the Trinity — Father, Son and Spirit — come to know themselves as unique, distinct Persons who are united in passionate self-emptying love. In joyful surrender to one another, the Father and the Son discover their uniqueness in their oneness through the hidden, emptying Spirit of Love.

By creating us according to His own image and likeness, God wishes to share His passionate self-emptying love with us. He also wishes to receive from us our return of such ecstatic love so that He may joyfully discover in His infinite humility still more His uniqueness as God who is love. This is the awesome "good news." God wished not only to share by giving His personalized love of Himself to us individually through Jesus Christ, but to wait patiently for us to return a self-giving of ourselves to Him in love.

What most of us have forgotten is that God wants our love and is affected by it. If God — as a triune community — is love, this means that within the Trinity the three Persons experience each other in a mutual giving and receiving, in an inter-change of self-gifts. They are "affected" by the gift of each other given in love. In a way, the Persons of the Trinity are continuously being "birthed" into their unique personhood in the silent, surrendering love of each other.

If such felt experiences are at the heart of God as loving community, must we not believe that the same giving and receiving in a felt experience of love is part of the Trinity's relationship to us? That God wills to love us means that He wills to give Himself completely to us as Jesus on the cross demonstrates. This should also mean that God wishes to receive our returned love. Love that is merely giving, but not receiving, is not true love for it is not affectively experienced.

Why Love?

WHY IS love necessary? Why should we love God and our neighbor? Is it in order to "save our soul," to do God's will and keep His commands? Do I love you and God in order to go to Heaven? We might ask: why does God the Father love you and me? Does His love admit of a reason beyond the mere act of being love? No. True love is never subservient to any other reason. God loves just because He loves. It is the ultimate, self-contained reason. Love is the ultimate reason for its own existence.

If I loved you for some reason, would that be true love? If God loved you and me for any reason, He would not be love by nature. God and we love, therefore, for no other "reason" than to be a self-surrendering gift to each other. If any human being loves another to gain money, sexual plea-sure or for any other motive of this sort, such love is a prostitution and in no way can it be called love. If we make love subservient to anything else, we introduce noise into our love and destroy the silence which is the language of self-emptying love. We revert to the deepest isolation even though we may be physically close to another. True love, even when words are used to express it, will always breathe the silence of the Trinity.

We are called to love God and other human beings as Jesus has loved us. And He loves us as the Father loves us (Jn 15:9). He loves our uniqueness, that which makes us different from any other person. Such love, as He showed us, made Him ready, for our sake and for no other reason, to lay down His life on the cross (Jn 15:13).

But we love, too, in order to receive. It is no selfish desire for a "thing." There can only be the passionate desire to receive one's true being in the union of true love. This is the basic need that even God "needs" that introduces unselfishness and humility into true love. Such a need for God or another beloved human being can never be seen as anything less than a humble plea to allow someone to bring us into a new realization of our true self through the gentle power of the Spirit.

An Incarnation Of God's Love

THE UNIQUENESS of Christianity is summed up in a brief but beautiful statement found in the first epistle of St. John:

> *No one has ever seen God;*
> *but as long as we love one another*
> *God will live in us*
> *and his love will be complete in us.*
> *We can know that we are living in him*
> *and he is living in us*
> *because he lets us share his Spirit. . .*
> *God is love*
> *and anyone who lives in love lives in God,*
> *and God lives in Him (1 Jn 4:12-13, 16).*

Although God, Father, Son and Spirit, dwells within us and loves us with an unchanging, infinitely perfect, self-giving love, such a love needs to become incarnated in order that we can humanly experience it. The incarnate Son of God, Jesus Christ, is the fullness of God's "unveiling" love as He hangs on the cross, emptied of self — poured out to the last drop of blood. Yet by His resurrectional presence, living within us, He "enfleshes" and makes incarnate again the triune God's love whenever we love in His Spirit.

The Spirit of Jesus in our hearts allows us, not only to experience the Father and the Son's presence as loving us, but He impels us in the power of that great love to love other human beings with God's universal love. To the degree that in prayer we become silent and listen to God's infinite love for us, to that degree God's Spirit turns us outward toward others to be a listening love to them. It is all "because the love of Christ overwhelms us" (2 Cor 5:14). This Spirit of Jesus silences us on the physical, psychical and spiritual levels so that we become integrated, whole persons.

We move beyond the fears and dark anxieties that prevent us from truly letting go and loving others and receiving their love in return. A freeing process in our loving encounters with other human beings takes place as we surrender ourselves to God's will. It is this state of abandonment to God's holy will that prompted St. Augustine to exclaim: "Love God and do whatever you wish."

To love as Jesus loves is not a license to love others according to our own insecure needs, driven by *eros* or our own selfish pleasures. It calls us to be "recollected" in God's loving presence, to be quick "to put to death anything in our nature which is rooted in earth" (Col 3:5).

Silent Love For Others

TRUE LOVE for God brings forth an intense and strong love for others. As we grow in greater awareness of the indwelling essence in the deepest center of our being, at the same time we become conscious of this divine, loving presence in, surrounding and penetrating all other things. The same energizing, loving God, experienced within, is seen in each creature met along the road of life. All such gifts from God show forth, "unveil" a bit of His beauty, and proclaim to us that God is "inside" His gifts. Touching them, we touch the Giver and adore Him. We surrender to His loving presence when we encounter it in the incarnation of each moment in matter.

Yet we need silence and solitude in order to recognize God as the Center of our being and the being of all other creatures. Especially is this true if we are to discover their unique "logos" or personhood in the *Logos* of God, Jesus Christ, according to whom all human beings have been made.

Henri Nouwen expresses it well: "Solitude and community belong together; each requires the other as do the centre and circumference of a circle. Solitude without community leads us to loneliness and despair but community without solitude hurls us into a 'void of words and feelings' (Bonhoeffer)." Such inner silence and solitude help us to dissipate any anxious, aggressive, noisy impulses to dominate each situation to satisfy our own physical and psychic needs. God's loving presence shines diaphanously even through the weaknesses and limitations of the other.

Knowing this enables us to accept honestly our own weaknesses and brokenness. Jean Vanier, the founder of *L'Arche*, loving communities of service to handicapped persons, writes of the solitude that brings such knowledge:

I discover more and more each day my need for these times of solitude in which I can rediscover others with more truth and accept, in the light of God, my own weakness, ignorance, egoism and fear. This solitude does not separate me from others; it helps me love them more tenderly, realistically and attentively. I begin to distinguish too between the false solitude which is a flight from others to be alone with egoism, sadness or a bruised sensitivity and the true solitude which is communion with God and others (Community and Growth, *pp. 118-19*).

Two Becoming One In Christ

ONLY GOD'S SPIRIT can infuse into our hearts true Christian love which is unselfish, humble and serving, for it is only God's Spirit who pours into our hearts the love of God (Rm 5:5). The more our love for other human beings comes from the Spirit, the more we seek the great privilege of serving them rather than our own selfish needs. Such Christ-love widens the circle beyond the immediate community of any given *I-Thou* to partake of a universal love that opens out to all men and women. It takes on the gentleness of a loving mother who seeks only to serve by bringing out the God-potential in each one we meet.

We go out from God the Center of all love. He has shown us how to let that love transform us into loving servants to the whole world. But we also go out from and return to those precious few loving communities where we most experience oneness and uniqueness. When we are rooted in God and in the love of at least one other human being who really incarnates His love for us and for the world, we are not torn between two separate and opposing centers. Quite the contrary. These two centers are mutually encompassing, the human and the divine milieux blending with each other and revealing each other to us.

When my friend and I both seek to surrender ourselves to God in a deep silence and solitude, God's silence touches our mutual silence. Solitude is not loneliness when it is shared, but the essence of community. We know that only God's silent Spirit can teach us how to love each other. To the degree that we can abandon ourselves to listen to God's Word spoken to us both as the Spirit of love builds us up into a oneness, into a community, to that degree do we discover from God how to avoid selfishness and yet how to progress to ever increasing, intense levels of love for each other. We also learn in our mutual love to discover God's uncreated energies of love, unfolding in the very "enfolding" of the two of us. Each encounter is like a new discovery of God, loving and revealing Himself through our mutual love for each other. Both of us discover God's self-revelation through His Word which is silently being spoken and recognized in the very words we utter in love to each other. We truly understand that "love comes from God and everyone who loves is begotten by God and knows God" (1 Jn 4:7).

Such love may reach a unique level between two persons. Yet, rooted in God, it can never become limiting and possessively exclusive. Each person is freed by the other to be a similar incarnation of God's love for many others. Each has, in such a friendship, experienced the joy of surrendering to God with the other and finds it easy to be open to ever increasing and widening circles of friends.

Dangerous Noises

LOVE, as pointed out, is not for sale, cannot be purchased, serves no other purpose than in and for itself if it is of God. We do not love in order to "get" to Heaven. We do not love each other for what we individually can receive from the other. True love is never an instrument to be used for some other purpose. Jesus gave us the two great commandments to love God and love our neighbor as we love ourselves as the summary of why God created us. If we have been created then, out of love of God and love of each other, why should that which is so important in God and our own lives, so essential and without which both God and we could never be or become our true selves, bring us so much pain and suffering? Do you really wish to love someone? Then be prepared to suffer! Why is this so?

As we learn both in union with God and friend to take the risk of opening ourselves to the other, we begin to experience fears and doubts. We open up areas of ourselves unknown to us before. Danger signs rise up along the way. Which way, Lord? How should we enflesh our love for one another? What should we do and how should we say it? Above all, we find a true confrontation with unredeemed, hidden areas of ourselves that surface as we see ourselves being mirrored in the openness of the other. Demands for sensitivity and fidelity not known before are made in proportion as we accept the gift of the other. Self can no longer be the center as we humbly and honestly seek to live and serve God in the uniqueness of the other. Noises from within rise up out of our selfishness to destroy the solitude and silence necessary to build a community in love. Teilhard de Chardin in his *The Divine Milieu* well expresses what happens as we "descend" beyond such superficial and personal control over others:

> *We must try to penetrate our most secret self, and examine our being from all sides. Let us try, patiently, to perceive the ocean of forces to which we are subjected and in which our growth is, as it were, steeped. . . And so, for the first time in my life perhaps (although I am supposed to meditate every day!), I took the lamp and, leaving the zone of everyday occupations and relationships*

where everything seems clear, I went down into my inmost self, to the deep abyss whence I feel dimly that my power of action emanates. But as I moved further and further away from the conventional certainties by which social life is superficially illuminated, I became aware that I was losing contact with myself. At each step of the descent a new person was disclosed within me of whose name I was no longer sure, and who no longer obeyed me. And when I had to stop my exploration because the path faded from beneath my steps, I found a bottomless abyss at my feet. . . At that moment . . . I felt the distress characteristic of a particle adrift in the universe, the distress which makes human wills founder daily under the crushing number of living things and stars. And if someone saved me, it was hearing the voice of the Gospel . . . speaking to me, from the depth of the night: ego sum, noli timere *(It is I, be not afraid). (pp. 76-8).*

Passover Experience

MOSES, COMING to the Red Sea, must have hesitated, at least for a moment, as he tried to decide whether he should lead the Israelites into the water and hope the waves would part or whether he should wait for the waters to part before plunging into the sea. How easy it is for us, too, to hesitate in the face of our human loves. The demands may be too great, the sacrifices far too many. The desert of so many unknown and mysterious factors challenges us. Life seemed so simple once, when we were in control. But now the call to be silent in the desert of our inner poverty and to listen in love to the needs of others threatens our security. The familiar, our long-time control over the situation, is no longer a luxury we enjoy. To have reached a oneness with another in God is to taste a bit of Heaven. But it is also to taste a bit of hell in terms of personal suffering. What agony to let go and not hold on to the other! Any separation from the one loved is, at best, a wrenching experience. And when the two are together how tempting to want the other to measure up to our own expectations. In the Spirit, though, we are gifted to love the other in faith and hope with something of the qualities of God's love for us.

So many of our sufferings in loving another come especially from the constant call to live in silent and solitary hope in the other, even when the substance hoped for is not yet to be found in the other. The one loved has not yet experienced himself or herself as good, noble or beautiful, yet we are expected to see the loved one as all of these things and more. Selfishness, though, can cause us to lose the sense of wonder and mystery, poetry and going beyond to live in the tremulous hope of the not-yet. We can't demand that the other person live up to our own noisy, self-centered dictates. Such lack of hope makes true love impossible. It is a return into isolation. Even worse, it is a foretaste of the essence of hell. We have begun to experience the *passover*. We have started to leave our isolation and to pass through trials and tribulations in the desert into a new degree of intimacy with another. In that union we discover a new oneness in God through deeper faith, hope and love. We hang suspended in the precarious moment of decision and no one — not the loved one, not God, not even any creature — can force us to cross over, or make our decision for us: to love or not to love. Like Hamlet, we hold our destiny in indecisive hands. What will our future be? One of selfishness? Or one of love?

Martin Buber in his work, *I and Thou*, presents us with an Hasidic parable:

> *(He) sat among peasants in a village inn and listened to their conversation. Then he heard how one asked the other, "Do you love me?" And the latter answered, "Now, of course, I love you very much." But the first regarded him sadly and reproached him for such words: "How can you say you love me? Do you know, then, my*

*faults?" And then the other fell silent, and silent they sat facing
each other, for there was nothing more to say. He who truly loves
knows, from the depths of his identity with the other, from the root
ground of the other's being, he knows where his friend is wanting.
This alone is love (p. 248).*

Patience is the love of God operating in us to give us
hope that out of such imperfections something very beautiful can result. It means foregoing our aggressive spirit to
pierce in silence beyond the threatening surface to the
"solitary" place where God transforms the imperfections of
the one loved by the patient love of God in the lover. What
creative and humble power the lover exercises as he or she
gives hope to the beloved that the latter is already beautiful
and can be more beautiful still. Such a true lover wishes to
serve that dream of the not-yet and give it creative substance. It is to enflesh God's love on earth again. It is to
unveil His very own beauty as one of His children, made in
His own image and likeness. It reflects His faith, hope and
love for two people who become progressively more one
with each other and with God. God's love is most released
and materialized in those patient struggles which demand
hope, the hope which alone can bring forth true love out of
such dark and silent struggles to "pass-over."

Rejected Love

IF WE HAVE the courage to take the first step into the solitude
and silence that true love requires, we will be called also to
enter into a similar aloneness with God's Spirit in the event
of experiencing our love rejected by our beloved. The Spirit
brings us to an inner freedom that results from our dying to
our false egos to be open in gentle receptivity to God speaking His Word in our friend. This freedom and total attach-

ment to the Lord show themselves in a humility which is able to sublimate any threatening pride and self-sufficiency and express in look and word that we are in need of others to bring us forth into new being.

Such freedom allows us to give ourselves in hopeful trust that the other will accept us. Our total availability opens us up to the pain of possibly being refused and wounded by others whom we have loved. In the gentleness of God's Spirit who helps us to control our isolated, inflated egos, we are able to transcend such hurts. The cross of Christ can often be most deeply experienced in what God has meant to be the most beautiful of human experiences.

Only God's Spirit can free us from the pain of rejection and enable us to seek humbly to be led by the same Spirit to offer ourselves again and again to others, as Jesus Himself did, in unselfish love. The pain and risk involved cannot compare to the healing joy of finding in another human being the presence of God, loving us and calling both of us into a greater union with Him and with each other.

Prayer As Love

THE SAME SPIRIT who pours God's love into our hearts teaches us in our weakness how to pray as we ought (Rm 8:26). We learn to love in greater consciousness of God's indwelling presence shining forth from the center of our loved one's being. To the degree that we can let God be present and love us at the center of our *I*, to that degree we can allow Him to lead us to the center of our friend's true being.

Gradually we see in true human love that our attitudes toward others change. Our approach toward God and prayer also changes. As we live in love for God and neighbor, so we pray. Prayer becomes a yielding to God's love and the love of our friends. It becomes a peaceful, joyful urge to surrender more totally to His presence within us and within our friends. We wish to live only to serve others.

Gone are the forceful, nervous outbursts that once high-lighted both our prayer before God and our encounters with our loved ones. Gentleness and patience and a joyful expectancy now characterize both our prayer and our loving encounters with others. We listen on a deeper level. Our focus is oriented toward the other. No longer is it trained on ourselves. We respect the other's uniqueness. We "strain forward" to see ways of serving that inner beauty and dignity locked inside the other.

We can apply to love and prayer what T.S. Eliot in *East Coker* expresses as the paradox of love and waiting in hope:

> *I said to my soul, be still, and wait without hope*
> *For hope would be hope for the wrong thing; wait without love*
> *For love would be love for the wrong thing; there is yet faith*
> *But the faith and the love and the hope are all in the waiting,*
> *Wait without thought, for you are not ready for thought:*
> *So the darkness shall be light, and the stillness the dancing*
> (Four Quartets, *p. 15*).

Love Is Caring

As we learn to listen in loving silence and waiting ex-pectancy for God to speak His Logos from the depths of the one we love, we discover that our love becomes purified and shows itself in deeper caring for the other. The caring of Jesus becomes our caring as we reach out to cover, protect, warm, bring into being the other's uniqueness. This is the caring that highlights the strange paradox that Jesus taught. Only when we lose our lives do we gain them in a new way (Lk 17:33). In showing loving care for another, God's love in us is released and incarnated on earth again as it was in Jesus.

But if we turn away in isolated uncaring for others, we turn towards darkness and non-entity. Hell is the state of non-identity of a true *I* in relation to a *Thou.* Rollo May expresses this fundamental truth of our human existence in this way:

> *When we do not care, we lose our being; and care is the way back to being. If I care about being, I will shepherd it with some attention paid to its welfare, whereas if I do not care, my being disintegrates* (Love and Will, *p. 290*).

Freed To Love

THE DEGREE of caring we show to others indicates the level of personal freedom and integration attained through Christ's Spirit. We are set free from all the obstacles that keep us in selfish isolation and unconcerned indifference toward others. The Spirit frees us from any selfish manipulating or unconcerned treatment of others, even should we believe such actions to be loving.

True freedom is never a static quality that allows us merely not to be coerced from outside, forcing us to choose between good or evil. It is a dynamic discovery of our true self as we freely in the power of God's Spirit take our life, our very person, and surrender it unresistingly back to God in order to be more loving of and giving of self to others. St. Paul clearly shows what true freedom means in terms of such love for others:

> *There must be no competition among you, no conceit; but everybody is to be self-effacing. Always consider the other person to be better than yourself, so that nobody thinks of his own interests first but everybody thinks of other people's interests instead (Ph 2:3-4).*

Turned Toward The World

OUR OPENNESS to others in the world is the continued work of the Holy Spirit. True love toward God never can be satisfied with mere resting in the indwelling presence of God. Nor can genuine love for another human being result in a selfish "a deux" that only intensifies one's selfishness and isolation. It would be tragic and conducive to greater unhappiness if two persons, especially a married couple, in the name of intimate love, would insulate themselves behind high psychic walls, built to keep them locked up within themselves and away from a world of unknown others.

Christianity teaches that love builds community, eventually unifying the entire world into the Body of Christ, the Church. But Christianity offers us human beings more than teaching. We are given hope in the power of Jesus, the risen Lord, who can conquer all sin and death. With such power intimately present to us through Christ's indwelling presence within us, we firmly believe and act upon this belief. Christ's love, transforming our own love, also in and through our loving service of others, can transform any and all brokenness and meaningless self-centered concerns. We no longer approach human situations relying solely on our own power. We learn to surrender in inner silence to God's immanent and transforming love in each happening. We become deeply aware of the everlasting repercussions of the least of our acts done out of unselfish love toward others, especially the neediest of this world. This is our Christian belief:

> And the King will answer, "I tell you solemnly, in so far as you did this to one of the least of these brothers of mine, you did it to me."
> ". . . I tell you solemnly, in so far as you neglected to do this to one of

*the least of these, you neglected to do it to me." And they will go
away to eternal punishment, and the virtuous to eternal life (Mt
25:40, 45-46).*

We go about our daily lives filled with child-like hope
and love, eager to use our gifts and talents for the good of
those whom we encounter. Such an approach to life goes
beyond every vision of loving union that we could imagine.
"The whole creation is eagerly waiting for God to reveal his
sons" (Rm 8:19). No longer do we cling to our own dreams,
but in silent adoration, in eucharistic worship we recognize
that we are not our own. We belong to another. We hear
God's word say to us about us: "This is My Body!"

Love is a call to beget new life. It breathes hope in what
may seem to be a hopeless situation. It asks only to be a
reconciler. It brings peace and joy where once there was but
chaos and sadness. It seeks to transform hatred into love.
The loving Christian, in touch with God's Word by silent
listening in each moment to the mind of Christ, learns the
excitement of surrendering to His Word, Jesus Christ. He
or she lives as a transforming reconciler to bring all things
into one in Christ through loving service.

*And for anyone who is in Christ, there is a new creation; the old
creation has gone, and now the new one is here. It is all God's work.
It was God who reconciled us to himself through Christ and gave us
the work of handing on this reconciliation. . . So we are ambassadors for Christ; it is as though God were appealing through us,
and the appeal that we make in Christ's name is: be reconciled to
God (2 Cor 5:17-20).*

CHAPTER EIGHT

The Silence Of The Body

WE SPEAK of the ever increasing levels of noise about us, especially in our cities where the majority of us live. Recently there was a newspaper account of what most Long Islanders in New York mistook for a rare Long Island earthquake. Scores of people saw their doors vibrate and their dishes rattle. It turned out to be merely a powerful sonic boom from one or more high-speed jets flying northeastward over Long Island from New Jersey!

Most of us, however, are unaware of the noises that exist within our bodies. These noises cannot be measured in decibels. They can only be seen in terms of warring dichotomies set up as our bodies fight our souls which attack our spirits. We have accepted a false opposition from early Platonic Christian writers between our physical bodies and our spiritual souls. Consciously or unconsciously we often denigrate our bodies and give too high a priority to our minds.

Too many of us, in Western Christianity, have difficulty accepting the fact that God created all of us as unified persons. We do not "have" a body or a soul. But we "are" embodied beings. We are ensouled and enspirited human persons. True salvation includes our total health and integration, therefore, as whole persons on all three levels of body, soul and spirit. The Jewish mind could never separate the person from his or her body, soul or spirit. The body is always possessed for it is through our body relationships that we are "situated" in place and time. "Body-ness" refers in Jewish thinking, not to an objective entity that we have and lose in death, but to the whole person in his or her state of transitoriness. When the Psalmist says that his "flesh" longs for God (Ps 63:1; 84:3), he is referring to his whole being, to the whole of his person which he recognizes to be an ephemeral entity in contrast to the everlasting Spirit of God.

St. Paul seems to have understood this well when he wrote: "May the God of peace make you perfect and holy; and may you all be kept safe and blameless, spirit, soul and body, for the coming of our Lord Jesus Christ" (1 Th 5:23). Through our bodies we become present to God, our neighbors, all the material cosmos and thus it is through our bodies that we grow in higher relationships of soul and spirit. The body is, therefore, not merely an object with which we are confronted. It is a way of our existing in this material world.

Yet through faulty teaching — alas, only all too often from Christian teachers — we have not only accepted such a separation between body, soul and spirit, but, even worse, we have acted at times with a kind of disdain toward the body. Dr. Paul Tournier, a Swiss medical doctor and Protestant lay theologian, describes this Western approach: "All the churches speak of incarnation, but they generally suggest a contempt for the body, as if the spirit had debased itself instead of fulfilled itself in this wonderful venture that God has willed. We find in all our patients, especially in our pious patients, a certain contempt for the body" (*The Meaning of the Body*).

True Incarnation

MANY OF OUR individual sicknesses and much of the disintegration of the personality that we see around us stems, in my opinion, from this most unhealthy separation between our *body* and our higher levels of *soul* and *spirit*. This means that we have not taken seriously the Incarnation, the fact that God so loves this material world, that His Word took on flesh and dwelt amongst us. Jesus Christ has assumed everything in His body that we possess as materialized beings, located in space and time.

Ludwig Feuerbach rather bluntly criticizes an abstract God of our mind against the real God in Christ incarnate: "The God in your head is gas and wind; the God in Christ is a fixed and solid body" (*The Essence of Faith According to Luther*, p. 71).

It is true, both from what Scripture reveals to us and from our daily experiences, that sin or the turning inward in egocentricism and away from true, loving communal sharing has brought about a state of disintegration within our very beings. We do not listen to God any more than did Adam and Eve. Through sin they ran away, not only covering their "bodies" with fig leaves, but also covering their spiritual ears, so as not to hear Him speak His Word to them. God always speaks His loving word and gives us His Spirit to recognize what that Word communicates to us. He also empowers us to fulfill His commands. But through our failure to live properly integrated lives we have introduced into our "bodies" noise and disharmony, sickness and unhappiness unto the death of God's life within us.

It is in the light of the antithesis between ourselves as self-centered and disobedient children of God and our true selves as loving and obedient children of the Father, filled with His Spirit that St. Paul highlights the saving, healing power of Jesus Christ as Redeemer. Through the Incarnation, the Son of God broke through the barrier separating the realm of divinity and life from that of humanity and death, both physical and moral. Although personally sinless, Christ came "in a body as physical as any sinful body" (Rm 8:3). Christ took upon Himself our estrangement by becoming like us in all things, save sin (Heb 4:15). Although He was united intimately with the Father, and thus always true God even while being true man, Christ in His earthly existence was in some sense not fully one with His Father. By taking upon Himself our flesh (*sarx*) condition, He entered a humanity in a state of "unsalvation" which bore the sign of sin, namely, death (Rm 5:12).

Not only are we infected with sin and death, but the whole of creation has been touched by the power of sin. Man and the whole sub-human creation have been affected by the consequences of sin. Man and the cosmos share the same fate of being subjected to these effects such as suffering and death and cannot reach fulfillment without the Savior.

"From the beginning till now the entire creation, as we know, has been groaning in one great act of giving birth; and not only creation, but all of us who possess the first fruits of the Spirit, we too groan inwardly as we wait for our bodies to be set free" (Rm 8:22-23).

Yet God had mercy and sent His Son in the likeness of sinful flesh (Rm 8:3) to condemn sin in the flesh by dying on the cross and through His resurrection, to redeem the whole world from sin. Jesus Christ passes gloriously from the state of flesh (*sarx*) according to St. Paul's teaching, to that of spirit (*pneuma*). As long as Jesus was confined, as we are, to His human flesh, He was not able to share His divine life with other human beings. But after His glorious resurrection, He, "the last Adam, became a spirit imparting life" (1 Cor 15:45).

St. John also affirms that before Jesus died, He could not yet send us His Spirit (Jn 7:37). Jesus Christ would effect our redemption and, through us, also that of the whole universe by overcoming the flesh and subjecting it to the spirit. Christ first experienced the fruits of this redemption within His own flesh. He conquered death by the transforming glory of His resurrection in which His carnal condition, that is, the state of estrangement from God, was transformed by the fullness of the Spirit of God's life. Just as His humanity was an integral part of His way of touching human beings, so now, by the resurrection of that same human bodied being, the whole Christ can touch the bodiliness of us all and enable us to receive a new healing and wholeness in one with God's divine life. This reorientation will eventually lead to a full resurrection in the Spirit. The glorified body of Jesus thus becomes the source of the Spirit of eternal life.

The Good News proclaimed by the Apostles of Jesus and the early Christian community through their mutual love for each other and the entire world is that by the power of the Risen Jesus we are in the process of becoming healthy and whole individuals, restored or re-made according to God's own image and likeness that Jesus Christ is by nature and by the Incarnation.

Let's take an honest look at our bodies. Don't we often feel that on this level of our existence we are not what God means us to be? Do we ever get a gnawing sensation that we are not living according to our full body, soul and spirit potential? Don't we sometimes feel the disintegration of our bodily members? Is not the body often considered by us to be a drag to our intellectual and spiritual life rather than an integral part of our entire, true self? Think for a moment of the quality and the amount of food and drink that we pour into our bodies. This body, St. Paul tells us, is a temple of the Holy Spirit, holy and sacred (1 Cor 3:16). Yet how unwittingly we abuse it, exploit its powers in an undisciplined way, to get as much pleasure out of it as we can with very little awareness all the while that the body is not a tool to bring us pleasure but that we *are* our bodies! We cannot separate our bodies from the persons that we are. And as our bodies exist, so do our spirits and our souls. There is an intimate interdependence between all three.

Need Of Healing

THERE IS no human being living who does not have his or her share of brokenness. All of us at one time or another need healing on the body, soul and spirit levels. We all feel a certain disorientation within our members. Our bodies often bring us pain, exhaustion, a heaviness that was not meant to be when God created us. God speaks his healing Word to us in silence. And we listen when we discipline our bodies to accept His call to more abundant life. Yet how much noise within our bodies drowns out that Word within? Our minds bind us also with their distracting thoughts, even demonic temptations, their tenuous grasp on a very limited area of knowledge that so easily can pass into forgetfulness or error through age and emotional stress.

One of the greatest of these psychic enslavements is fear. It is the very opposite of faith. When we lack a healing experience of God's personal love for us, we lack a sense of our true identity in Christ and are easily overcome by fear. Fear is primarily centered in the apprehension of a past threat to our security or to a future danger that spawns other satellites of unhappiness, doubt, anxiety, worry, dread, hatred, danger, horror, fright or terror. Such thoughts of impending evil weigh heavily upon our psyches and our bodies, crippling our growth and breaking down our health.

Nearly 75% to 80% of all physical ills are reputedly connected to a disturbed psyche's debilitating effect on the body's natural defense against sicknesses and disease. And many of these disturbances are due to needless fear. Most doctors seek to treat the symptoms brought on by fear. But we must discover the root of fear which is often centered in a lack of faith and trust in God's loving care for us.

It was Dr. Carl Jung who wrote in 1932 about the need for a religious view to bring wholeness to the psyche. "Among my patients in the second half of life — that is to say over thirty-five — there has not been one whose problem in the last resort was not that of finding a religious outlook on life. It is safe to say that every one of them fell ill because he had lost that which the living religions of every age have given to their followers, and none on them has been really healed who has not regained this religious outlook" (*Modern Man in Search of a Soul*, p. 259).

For Christians, Jesus Christ is the Way that heals the world of its brokenness. He has come among us in order to bring us life, that we might have it more abundantly (Jn 10:10). He inserted Himself into our broken, human condition in order that He might prove how beautiful we are in His love, the imaged love of the Heavenly Father for all of us. Having such a healing faith in God's personal love for us unto death means to be caught up into an understanding greater than any intellectual grasp of a statement about God's love for us we could ever have. It is to be possessed of an inner power, infused into our spirit by the Holy Spirit of the risen Jesus, that shakes us out of our false, illusory world (Ep 4:17) and turns us toward the discovery of our true self in God's infinite love. It is such faith that transforms us and heals us and brings us into a new and eternal life that is already a sharing in the resurrection of the Lord.

But such healing on body-soul-spirit levels is an ongoing

process and depends upon the silent surrender of ourselves
to the guiding presence of the indwelling Trinity. This is
what the Gospels tell us about the healing power of Jesus.
He stretched out His healing hands and the sick felt the love
of God pour into their broken bodies, minds and hearts. He
was the Son of God and they, for a brief moment of infused
faith, hung suspended between the darkness of their own
isolation and the light of the truth that they were indeed
sons and daughters of God. They surrendered to the presence of Jesus' love in their lives and they felt whole for the
very first time. But they had to continue to listen to His
commands and obey them. They had to bring their "new
creation" in Christ to bear on their faulty ways of relating on
their body, soul and spirit levels.

That same Jesus goes about our present world, stretch-
ing out His hands of compassionate mercy and love, and
asking only that we, in our brokenness, believe that He is
infinite love incarnate, the Divine Physician, who alone can
heal us of all our sicknesses. "Go; your faith has saved
(healed) you" (Mk 10:52). A leper was healed because of his
faith in Jesus (Lk 17:19). Jesus told the woman suffering
from a hemorrhage: "My daughter, your faith has restored
you to health; go in peace and be free from your complaint"
(Mk 5:34).

As those characters of the Gospel surrendered their
disharmony and false selves to Jesus, their bodily ills, psychic
fears and personal guilts were lifted from them. Like
Lazarus who stepped out of the tomb into new life by the
power of Jesus, so they experienced the healing which came
from their surrender in faith to the Lord. We are a part of
those persons who met Jesus in their expectant faith. We
have the same opportunity to encounter Jesus alive today in
our lives if we have the discipline and continued desire to

listen in silence to His Word telling us what *we* must do to be healed.

Whole Persons

IF GOD is love, as revealed by Jesus Christ, then God wishes us to be whole persons, integrated, enjoying a full and abundant life and not living disintegrated lives in a state of more sickness than health. God loves us as whole persons. If He counts every hair on our heads (Lk 12:7), how much more importantly is He helping us toward fullness of health in our bodies? If Jesus told us not to fear and be overly anxious about things and events that pass into oblivion tomorrow, then He is bringing us the power of His Spirit to live in His perfect love that casts out all fear (1 Jn 4:18) in the present. If we are to become true, mature Christians we will give attention to each dimension of our existence for, on each level — bodily, psychic and spiritual — God calls us into a greater unity with Him and one another, and an awareness of our true identity in our uniqueness as individual persons.

Juvenal, the Roman poet, gave us the oft quoted statement: *"Mens sana in corpore sano"* ("A sound mind in a healthy body"). This can be reversed as those modern sciences which deal with the healing of body and psyche show us: "A sound body in a healthy mind." We could even say, "A healthy body in a healthy mind through a healthy spirit." The spirit is healthily rooted when it is consciously aware of God's indwelling presence as love. Jesus knew — as modern doctors and psychiatrists and preachers are beginning to know — that the body, soul and spirit interact in us and powerfully influence one another.

They cannot be considered like tightly concealed compartments of self-contained entities or as enemies warring against each other. We all have daily experience of the increasing stresses and anxieties that we must put up with. We know how such psychic strains powerfully affect our bodies. High blood pressure, heart condition, ulcers, allergies, arthritis, even stages of cancer development show a direct relationship between a disturbed psyche and certain somatic diseases and illnesses.

A Beautiful Self

IT IS on the spiritual level of our personal relationship with the triune God, Father, Son and Holy Spirit, that we are integrated and all our relationships healed. As Jesus was able to heal only a few persons in Nazareth because of His fellow-townsmen's lack of faith in Him (Mk 5:25), so we will never truly be able to experience the wholeness which comes from His healing touch except through faith. The spiritual in us is not a subordinate means to the goal of enjoying health of body and soul. Rather, physical and mental health are subordinate to the moral or spiritual plane.

In the broken situations of our daily living, Jesus asks us what He asked the sick and maimed who came to Him during His public ministry and sought healing two thousand years ago: "Do you believe I can heal you?" His Voice becomes increasingly louder as we silence our own and listen to His will for us. We experience in this deeper kind of prayer — where we live at the center of our being and find the triune God dwelling there as our ultimate Center — how beautiful we are in body, soul and spirit, how uniquely loved by God we are as persons and how uniquely able we are to be loving towards others. Not only do we listen with open bodies, souls and spirits, but also with a strong will to discipline ourselves to do whatever God's Voice tells us to do in keeping with human reason and the findings of science to keep ourselves well and healthy.

Desire For Health

WE ALL WANT to be healthy, above all, physically. How many of us would give anything to lose 15 or 20 pounds of unnecessary weight, to get rid of high blood pressure, arthritis, allergies, or ulcers! Who of us likes to pay exorbitant hospital and doctor's bills for operations and examinations? Above all, who likes to suffer physically, limping through life in more pain than not? Who enjoys living locked inside the prison of one's inner fears? How often our very ideas about health and happiness are built on illusions that do not get at the true causes of our illness and discontent. Medicine and surgery and the use of soothing psychic exercises to calm the troubled waters of the mind often leave the fears that are at the root of so much physical and psychic sicknesses untouched. What we also need is a spiritual conversion, an inner transformation of our lives through the healing power of faith in a personal, loving God.

Such a true healing begins as a part of an ongoing process as we confront courageously the brokenness within our own personal lives and around us in the various communities that fashion us into the persons we are. As part of our ongoing healing, God expects us to learn the inner discipline necessary to bring the body with all its needs and appetites into harmony with an enlightened soul and spirit. He wants to bring to us His peace and joy, fruit of the Holy Spirit through His love poured out into our hearts (Gal 5:22; Rm 5:5). Let us look at what we are being called by God to do in a process of disciplining our bodies in order that physically we can be totally surrendered to the indwelling Trinity who abides within us as a beautiful temple (1 Cor 3:16).

Unity Versus Fragmentation

TODAY WE SEE a great return to holistic healing in the West. It is a return to the vision of healing once held by the pioneers of the healing profession as we know it. Pythagoras, the teacher of Hippocrates who is considered the Father of modern medicine, insisted that health is harmony of life and disease is the loss of equilibrium. He also saw the interrelationship between food, peace of mind and physical health. Hippocrates saw medicine as the art of getting people to reform their lives.

Dr. Paul Tournier writes:

> . . . *today men of very different outlooks, doctors, lawyers, economists, scientists, writers, freethinkers, atheists, Jews, as well as Catholic and Protestant Christians, are searching for something completely new. For something which is not simply a prolongation of the cultural development of the last several centuries, but which will rather interrupt that development. For something which is not so much on the order of scientific analysis but is more on the order of intuitive analysis; for something which no longer fragments man but rather restores his unity* (The Whole Person in a Broken World, *Preface*).

The religion of Christ is one of healing, of overcoming by the power of God's Spirit the disharmony brought into God's original creation through sin. It aims at a unification and integration of the material, psychic and spiritual planes within us as human beings and then through us to restore such a unity to the cosmos. Church leaders are beginning to join medical and psychological specialists to stop the faulty thinking that sends people who are sick in body exclusively to medical doctors while those who are mentally ill go to psychiatrists and psychologists to be healed and those who are spiritually sick present themselves to priests and ministers to be reconciled in spirit with God. All three are needed.

Physical Silence

ONE OF THE greatest needs in our modern society today is to learn how to relax physically from all the strains, stresses and tensions that are brought on by our hyper-activism. We move at such a terrific pace during most of our waking, working hours. Our bodies become more tense, our muscles and nerves more taut as the day progresses. Our society, dominated on the one hand by puritanical notions of good and evil and on the other hand by a kind of compulsion to compete and excel, does not allow us to stop and smell the roses, to be quiet and, like children, to sense deeply the wonder of the present moment. As a result we never really get to know ourselves, never get to experience in any kind of profound sense the world immediately around us. Instead of being compelled to *do* frenetically, we must learn the secret of turning toward our inner Center where the Holy Spirit abides and there make contact with the source of our *being*. "Fear not, it is I!" We must learn ways to make connection with the living, dynamic flow of energy all around us and within us, the uncreated energies of God's love and to surrender to these creative powers. All of us are in need of a physical place and time, preferably early in the morning or before retiring, to which we can go and silence our busy bodies.

Christian Yoga

THOUSANDS OF YEARS before the advent of Christianity, Hindu mystics hit upon the need of relaxing the body to prepare the person for union with the divine. Today most of us have some introduction to the yogic postures, called *Hatha Yoga.* These are isometric exercises designed to gradually bring the entire body into a relaxed state which in turn exerts an integrating power over the psyche and the inner spirit. Before we enter into prayer, at least our own individual prayer, we should start with our bodies by seeking physical harmony and peace.

A way of become "one-pointed," suggested by yoga techniques, is to focus intently on a physical object placed before you such as a beautiful flower, a painting or a piece of sculpture. Focus upon it with all your senses. Try to devour it with your eyes. Listen to the music of its colors. Smell its special fragrance. Become immersed in the object so that soon the distance between you and the object is overcome, and you feel one with the thing you are contemplating. See how your mind has slowed down and moved away from a busy *doing* to a state of just being one with what you are admiring. Gradually, a feeling that admits of great intensity and growth allows you to transcend the tyranny of your "conditioned" self and the limitations of time, place and uncontrolled desires. This can be accomplished especially in your prayer before the Blessed Sacrament.

Through such disciplined concentration you will not only begin to perceive a oneness with the world outside you but also a slowing down of your own self-centered activities. This brings an accompanying sense of deep peace and integration, a feeling of becoming a whole person. This also can be attained by making use of the *mantra* so common in religions of the Far East, Christian and otherwise. The former center upon the chanting and then the silent, mental repetition of the name of Jesus that was synchronized with one's breathing. St. John Climacus in his *Ladder of Perfection* exhorts Christians: "May the memory of Jesus combine with your breathing; then you will understand the use of silence."

This simple prayer, much like the *Hail Mary* forming the Rosary in the West, was first repeated reverently with the lips, and then in the mind with greater concentration on the presence of the risen Lord within the contemplative. Finally the name of Jesus became centered in the heart, became fused with the total person praying. The senses, emotions, imagination, intellect and will all converged upon the intimate presence of the Lord. The idea was to move the "mind" into the "heart."

A Silent Home

TO THE DEGREE that we find our inner center where our consciousness meets God as our ultimate Center in loving adoration, so we extend our spirit to the environment of our home. Have you ever noticed how one's room, one's home, including the yard and garden, usually reflect the inner state of those who live there? When you are in harmony within your body, you take care to order your room and your home. Peace within generates peace without and all around. Wholeness begets wholeness, spiritual, physical and psychic.

What is the noise level where you live? Is there any lack of harmony in the kitchen, dining room, living room, bedroom, bath? Do too many pieces of furniture clutter up the space around you thus having the psychological effect of cluttering up your mind? A small but important thing is to place noise absorbers on the legs of tables and chairs. Locks and hinges should be well oiled. There should be strips of felt between doors and frames. Noise absorbing rugs are to be preferred to bare wooden or tile floors. You need to *want* silence before you can obtain it. The indiscriminate use of TV and stereo, especially by young children and teenagers in the family, can be especially disturbing to the peace of the house. Even though we may not be "tuned into" such noises, they still affect us on an unconscious level.

"Silent" Speech

ONLY ABOUT 30% of our ideas are communicated by means of words. Most of our talk conveys very little in terms of intellectual content. How often we babble on, without much control of our tongue or without much inner reflection on what we wish to say or should say. Much of our psychic dissipation comes through the misuse of our tongue. We are in most need of putting into practice St. Paul's advice to bring into captivity and in obedience to Jesus Christ every thought and every imagination (2 Cor 10:5). St. James' famous statement about controlling the tongue should help us to keep constant check on our uncontrolled verbosity.

> . . . the only man who could reach perfection would be someone who never said anything wrong — he would be able to control every part of himself. Once we put a bit into the horse's mouth, to make it do what we want, we have the whole animal under our control. Or think of the ships: no matter how big they are, even if a gale is driving them, the man at the helm can steer them anywhere he likes by controlling a tiny rudder. So is the tongue only a tiny part of the body, but it can proudly claim that it does great things. Think how small a flame can set fire to a huge forest; the tongue is a flame like that. Among all the parts of the body, the tongue is a whole wicked world in itself; it infects the whole body; catching fire itself from hell, it sets fire to the whole wheel of creation . . . but nobody can tame the tongue — it is a pest that will not keep still, full of deadly poison. We use it to bless the Lord and Father, but we also use it to curse men who are made in God's image; the blessing and the curse come out of the same mouth (Jm 3:2-10).

Isaiah writes: "Your salvation lay in conversion and tranquility; your strength, in complete trust" (Is 30:15). When we are grounded in silent prayer and living at the Center which is God indwelling us, then peace and tranquility flow over us. We find it easy to measure our words. Dante wrote, "A pithy saying feeds a great flame." When we bring each thought under Christ, then the words that enflesh that thought will radiate power. The words we speak will come from an inner divine energy, touching the hearts of those who listen to us. With the author of *Ecclesiastes* we will come to know that there is a time to keep silent and a time to speak (Qo 3:7). Discipline and self-control are the key to silencing our words.

This does not mean that we should feel guilty if we are called upon to speak. We can speak all day long and still maintain an inner silence, an economy of words, because our words flow from God's permissive will. Catherine de Hueck Doherty well describes such "silent" speaking:

> *A day filled with noise and voices can be a day of silence, if the noises become for us the echo of the presence of God, if the voices are, for us messages and solicitations of God. When we speak of ourselves and are filled with ourselves, we leave silence behind. When we repeat the intimate words of God that he has left within us, our silence remains intact* (Poustinia, p. 23).

Simplicity

THE SIMPLICITY of our words brings us into an honesty and truth that betray an inner oneness and purity of heart before the Lord. We seek only to do His will, to live in His Kingdom, to give Him glory and honor by every thought, word and deed. Jesus lived His earthly life in such simplicity, guided at all times by what would please His Heavenly

Father. He had that inner eye that was simple and gazing always upon the face of His Father. We have been made also to be simple as He was, in our words, our gestures, our thoughts, our actions, the possessions that surround us in our homes, the way we carry ourselves, the clothes we wear, the way we care for ourselves, the food we eat, the drink we consume. "God made man simple; man's complex problems are of his own devising" (Qo 7:30).

The Shaker Way brought to Christianity in America a simple approach to life in Christ. They proclaimed the presence of Christ in all creation through their reverence for it. They eschewed consumerism in all its forms from the very beginning. Theirs was a simple life:

> 'Tis a gift to be simple,
> 'Tis a gift to be free,
> 'Tis a gift to come down where we ought to be,
> And when we see ourselves in a way that's right,
> We will live in a valley of love and delight!
>
> When true simplicity is gained,
> To live and to love we will never be ashamed
> To turn and to turn will be our delight,
> Till by turning, turning, turning
> We turn 'round right.

Silent Gestures

OUT OF OUR SILENT CENTER, not only will our words come forth with deep power, unity and love but also the very comportment of our body and the manner in which we gesture. Seventy percent of our communication comes through body language, a look, a smiling glance, an up-curled lip, wrinkles on the forehead, fiery eyes smoldering with anger or dancing with joy.

When we see a recollected person, filled with reverence for God's presence within and without, we see a person with spontaneous, free movements, yet movements under control. When we see a person with *ataxia,* an inability to coordinate normally voluntary muscular movements, we judge that the person is affected with some muscular degenerative disease like multiple sclerosis or cerebral palsy or possibly that he is intoxicated.

I have always been edified by the controlled gestures of Japanese Buddhist monks as they go about their monastic tasks. Each movement is an extension of an inner reverence as they live at the divine Center within them. No wasted gesture, no unwarranted noise. All is harmony and silence. It's known as doing everything in the "Zen" way. We would call it doing all in a recollected manner, aware of God intimately present, "in whom we live and move and have our being" (Ac 17:28). How children, especially, need this silent discipline of bodily gesture and movement! Yes, even children can be taught to be contemplatives, to be reflective and recollected. Much depends on our example!

Food And Its Effect

FLYING AS MUCH AS I do gives me long hours to observe fellow passengers, especially children, a captive audience, an exploding volcano of energy and often just about as out of control. Surely the diet of modern Westerners today confirms what Ludwig Feuerbach wrote decades ago, namely: Man is what he eats! How many children, I wonder, are hyperactive on account of the sweets they eat. Sugars taken in excess have proven to have a specifically deleterious role in this respect. There is no longer any doubt that there is a close relationship between what we put into our mouths and how we feel physically and psychologically. Christianity exhorts us to eat and drink in moderation, in a sacramental way, in a way that will bring us into the presence of the indwelling God. The manner in which we eat is to be done in a prayerful uplifting of our minds and bodies to God in adoration and thanksgiving to the Giver of all gifts.

Aware of our great dignity to be a chosen temple in which God's Holy Spirit dwells with the Father and Son, we are exhorted to eat simple foods, foods that will induce harmony and peace. As a people, we Americans have the greatest variety of the very best food in the world. And yet we are not a healthy people. We stuff ourselves with much quantity, but often what we put into our mouths are empty calories. As I write this, I am reading an article in today's newspaper citing the fact that we spent $2 billion in 1984 alone on chemical pesticides and sprays. And this is only the urban population on their own private gardens. Yet we all know that such chemicals introduce into our bodies toxic poisons whose effects are still fully to be determined.

Dr. Carl E. Braaten, a theologian teaching on the faculty of the School of Divinity at the University of Chicago, gives some alarming statistics in his book, *The Living Temple*. We are not a healthy people because of what we eat and how we eat, viz. without much exercise and moderation. Americans spend $120 million annually on laxatives. In a year they consume 5000 tons of aspirin. Tons of sleeping pills, pep pills, tranquilizers, reducing pills and antacids are consumed, only to mask symptoms of something that troubles us far more deeply. One half million die of heart attacks each year while 27 million have some kind of heart condition. Over 7 million have some kind of arthritis or rheumatism. One out of ten men have a stomach ulcer. Millions suffer from diabetes or hypoglycemia, chronic disorders such as asthma, anemia, colitis, cancer, senility, mental and nervous diseases, alcoholism and respiratory difficulties. Twenty-five percent have a problem with obesity (pp. 31-32).

We need not merely to fill our stomachs three times a day but to eat a good nutritious diet with a proper balance of proteins, fats and carbohydrates, high in vitamins and minerals, especially those which come to us in purer form in raw fruits and vegetables which are naturally grown. Concretely what can be done in this matter to bring about a greater physical harmony of the body in union with a peaceful soul and spirit? (1) We can avoid "bad" foods that can be harmful to our total health, such as are many pre-packaged, synthetic foods. Nearly two-thirds of what we eat around the family table or in restaurants or hospitals in America today comes pre-packaged and often contains harmful quantities of salt, sugar, preservatives and colorings that are not only not nutritious but can be extremely bad for us if such is our constant diet. Avoid refined carbohydrates and white sugar products, saturated and hydrogenated fats, foods that contain high levels of sodium nitrates such as hot dogs and sausage, white flour products and sugared cereals. (2) Try to eat foods grown in an organic way, free from chemical fertilizers and sprays. (3) Prefer fresh fruits and vegetables and foods from whole grains. (4) Cut down on (but do not totally exclude) the quantity of meat you consume. Select fish, chicken and turkey rather than red meat as a rule. (5) Drink uncontaminated water that truly cleanses the body internally and supplies minerals that are often missing in city water. (6) Do not gulp down your food in haste. Eat when you can take your time to digest, in pleasant surroundings, the food you take. Do not wash down your food with liquids taken during the meal, but drink about an hour before the meal, or an hour and a half after you've eaten.

We are frequently "dis-eased" in the body because of the

junk food that we ingest thus upsetting our "inner ecology."
If there is no harmony in the body, there will never be that
inner harmony of our minds which contributes so to wholeness of body, soul and spirit.

The Role Of Fresh Air

SCIENTISTS HAVE BEEN giving us solid proof that many of our
respiratory problems are mainly the result of breathing in
smoke-filled air. They point out the countless harmful effects of smoking: cancer, emphysema, asthma, heart attacks, cardio-vascular problems of all kinds, etc., etc. People
who do not smoke themselves but are constantly exposed to
it at home or at work likewise breathe in a very large
percentage of these toxins which are so harmful to anyone's
physical health. As industries continue to belch their pollut-
ants into our city air and the cars and trucks and buses
contribute their share to the poisons in the atmosphere we
breathe, we are all of us made victims of progress. Fresh air,
like good food, is essential to our overall well being.

Fasting

THOUGH unsupervised fasting can be dangerous to one's
health, when done prudently and, if extreme, under a
doctor's care, it is one of the best ways I know of to tone up
the body and bring it into joyful harmony in the Spirit. Jesus
took it for granted that his disciples would fast regularly, but
He taught them not to be hypocritical and parade their
fasting exploits before others out of spiritual pride (Mt
6:16-18).

His followers seek to fast primarily as an act of worship to
God. It is creative suffering and is done for no other reason
than to celebrate God's love for them and to return that love

by sacrifice. It is frequently joined to petitional prayer on behalf of oneself or others. It is essential as an ongoing part of Christian *metanoia* or conversion where we enter into a state of inner listening to God and try to live our lives by the balance and truthfulness that is called humility. It is also one of the best ways to unite ourselves with the poor, the oppressed and the suffering of this world. For the starving millions on earth today, we can do little but try to express our solidarity with them by joining them in their physical hunger, entering into their discomfort with them and offering it to God on their behalf.

Fasting is a physical, bodily act by which we cut down on our usual in-take of food. There are all sorts of fasting. The "normal" fast consists in taking no solid food whatsoever. Other fasts might consist solely of liquids, such as fruit juices, or in the eating of only raw vegetables or fruit or bread. What is important is that there be a sense of hunger, of relying on the power of God, of a "pass-over" from weakness and want to strength and satiety. In fasting as in all things, moderation — whereby we attain a proper balance in the use of words, food, drink, sleep, work and play — must be the rule.

Liturgy

WE HAVE SPOKEN about disciplining the body unto silence in our individual comportment. There is a great need for us, as Christians, to understand the discipline of silence when we gather together in the worshipful prayer of the Liturgy. The Church teaches us through the bodily gestures, postures and actions of the celebrating priest and deacons along with the parishioners how silence and sound complement one another in our worship. For silence is nothing unless it is "uttered" as a response to what has been communicated within a loving community, worshiping, adoring and surrendering to Christ's Spirit.

Our Liturgy or Mass is made up of two main parts: the Liturgy of the Word and the Liturgy of the Eucharist. We are called to physical, psychic and spiritual silence as with inner attention we are instructed in the Liturgy of the Word in Christ's values, according to the way He lived. Then in the Liturgy of the Eucharist we are empowered to put these values into action through the Holy Spirit who unites us all through Christ into His one Body.

In Christian worship, therefore, we see the model for our entire life outside of formal prayer. We learn how to bring together into a complementarity both silence and sound, a listening and a response. Thus throughout the Liturgy we are asked to be physically silent, as for example, during our listening to the Word both as it is proclaimed by the readers and preached by the homilist. A period of silent reflection should follow as we ponder the Word's meaning for us as a community and as individuals.

Then there are times when, without breaking our inner silence, we make a sound, a response to the triune God who has spoken to us in silence. At times this response is one of joy and celebration and comes out of the silence in which we reflected upon the Good News that we heard. The Psalmist invites us: "Clap your hands, all you peoples, acclaim God with shouts of joy" (Ps 47:1). Such sounds in music and/or dance do not oppose our silence but complement it as a fitting response while we remain centered in silence. Celebration calls for physical expressions of joy and enthusiasm because of what has been experienced in the silence of adoration.

The Liturgy teaches us many physical postures for praying. At times we are called, as pilgrims, to stand attentively and silently to hear the Word proclaimed. At other times we are asked to sit in a relaxed manner to accept God's presence in joyful celebration. At times we kneel in adoration at the moments that call for our greatest reverence, as at the consecration and after receiving the Eucharist. Eastern Christianity has brought to the West a freedom in other bodily positions in liturgical prayer as well, such as prostration out of a spirit of compunction, of making the sign of the cross in honor of the Trinity, of holding the hands, palms up and raised aloft toward Heaven. But all gestures and positions of the body in liturgical prayer are useful only insofar as they favor deeper prayer on the part of the individual.

Continued Conversion

ALL OF WHAT has been written in this chapter can be summarized by Christ's call of us to a continued conversion to become like unto little children. He said: "I tell you solemnly, unless you change and become like little children you will never enter the kingdom of heaven. And so, the one who makes himself as little as this little child is the greatest in the kingdom of heaven" (Mt 18:3-4).

Jesus is asking us, His disciples, to turn away from self-centeredness by a *metanoia* or inner conversion. In Greek this word means that one have a complete turnabout in attitude and consciousness. The values by which we live must now be centered completely on God as manifested through the workings of God's Word, Jesus Christ. St. Paul calls it a "spiritual revolution" (Ep 4:23). Jesus Himself insisted that we must be "reborn" of His Spirit or we cannot enter the kingdom of God (Jn 3:3, 5).

Such a continued conversion embraces at the same time our body-soul-spirit relationships. A child, two years old, exhibits qualities that Jesus must have had in mind when He held little children up to us as a model of conversion: trust and a readiness to obey the parent without fear. A little child is full of confidence in the love of the parent. In fact, docility and confidence are its main strengths. "Enough for me to keep my soul tranquil and quiet like a child in its mother's arms, as content as a child that has been weaned" (Ps 131:2).

An adult, to become spiritually such a child, must be a great person, mature and very much "together." It takes courage and perseverance to become like such a little child. It is demanding to live in the silence of the body which leads to the silence of the soul and spirit as an individual becomes whole, a true child of God, totally turned to the Heavenly Father in union with Christ through His Spirit and able to cry out on all levels of his or her being: "Abba, Father!" (Rm 8:16).

CHAPTER NINE

Christ-Mindedness

YEARS AGO I read a story about a Christian monk who lived in the fourth century as a hermit in the desert. A robber stole from him the few coins which the hermit had and fled. A short time later the hermit discovered a few other coins which the robber had evidently overlooked. He rushed off after the thief and joyfully gave these last few coins to him as if the robber were doing the hermit a great favor by relieving the holy man of all of his material possessions. That story has always been for me a "part-time" *koan*, a conundrum that hides more than it reveals but which, when reflected on, proves to be very rich in wisdom.

I kept asking myself: why did the hermit run after the robber and give him all the money that he had? But, in pondering the Gospel narrative, I added to the monk's story another about the widow who placed her last coins into the Temple treasury. Jesus said to His disciples on that occasion: "I tell you truly, this poor widow has put in more than any of them; for these have all contributed money they had over, but she from the little she had has put in all she had to live on" (Lk 21:3-4). Why did the widow put into the treasury all she had?

The same *koan* keeps popping up in the Gospel. Why did God give us everything He had in Jesus? Why did Jesus die for us shedding the very last drop of His own blood? Are all of these impractical tales about a simpleton monk, a mentally irresponsible widow, Jesus' self-giving and His Sermon on the Mount (Mt 5:1-12; Lk 6:20-23, 27-38) only examples of some kind of Oriental hyperbole? For years I have struggled with these conundrums which, when approached with human reasoning alone, seemed to have so little application to our modern living situation. Little by little, though, I began to realize the depth of truth that was veiled by their very simplicity. It was something that Jesus tried to teach us in the many paradoxes of the Gospel and which St. Francis of Assisi had come to understand so well when he penned his famous prayer: "It is in giving that we receive; it is in pardoning that we are pardoned; and it is in dying that we're born to eternal life."

By His death and resurrection, Jesus has conquered the forces of evil and made us into a new creation. Through the infusion of the gifts of deeper faith, hope and love, His Spirit gives us a new perception of reality. Our thinking and our acting take on a whole new, spiritual dimension as we "put on the Lord Jesus Christ" (Rm 13:14). St. Paul talked about this mystery of our transformation when he wrote:

That is why you must kill everything in you that belongs only to earthly life: fornication, impurity, guilty passion, evil desires and especially greed, which is the same thing as worshipping a false god; all this is the sort of behavior that makes God angry. And it is the way in which you used to live when you were surrounded by people doing the same thing; but now you, of all people, must give all these things up: getting angry, being bad-tempered, spitefulness, abusive language and dirty talk; and never tell each other lies. You have stripped off your old behavior with your old self, and you have put on a new self which will progress towards true knowledge the more it is renewed in the image of its creator, and in that image there is no room for distinction between Greek and Jew,

> *between the circumcised or the uncircumcised, or between barbarian and Scythian, slave and free man. There is only Christ: he is everything and he is in everything (Col 3:5-11).*

Totally Human

WHEN GOD GAVE us His Son to become one of us, that Son "emptied himself to assume the condition of a slave, and became as men are; and being as all men are, he was humbler yet, even to accepting death, death on a cross" (Ph 2:7-8). Jesus, the radiant Light of the Father's reflected glory, consented to assume the condition of Adam and all other human beings who by sin become slaves to their own false selves. Adam failed to become what God had destined him to be — a loving child of God by grace. He wanted to possess His human nature independently of God as though he were a god himself.

But Jesus took on the form of a suffering servant. He entered into our darkened world, was born into a blood line whose ancestors numbered idolaters and kings, prophets and patriarchs, murderers, adulterers and saints. He consented to be tempted in all things, but He did not sin (Heb 4:15). He never claimed His natural, divine right to rule the world, but He gained the whole world from His Father by fulfilling His Father's will in the most perfect manner possible, making Himself obedient unto death, even death on the cross out of love for us. Jesus not only taught the world this paradox of the Gospel but He lived out this basic truth that possessiveness of life, things, other persons, and even of God, destroys, while only love as expressed in total self-giving heals, liberates and brings happiness that will last forever.

His conviction of the correctness of His approach stemmed from His constant conscious awareness of the spiritual dimension of all life. It was the truth which led the way to eternal life. It was the Father's Truth, the Father's Way, the Father's Life. This is the way the Father thinks and acts and lives. And because Jesus so perfectly exemplified the Father, He could say of Himself and mean it, "I am the Way, the Truth and the Life" (Jn 14:6).

Love always requires an emptying if one is to give oneself to another. God is love. He loves us with a passion, the passion of Jesus. In Jesus' total submission to the point where He no longer possessed anything of His own to prove His love for us, Jesus showed us the depth of the Father's infinite love.

When our Lord became a little child, He exposed the weakness of God. No Father is strong before the cry of his needy child. God became vulnerable the day He let us call Him Father. We can hurt Him just as man hurt Jesus through rejection and indifference. For us Christians, Christ images a wisdom beyond mere human understanding. St. Paul wrote to the Corinthians that the Jews were seeking miracles and the Greeks were looking for wisdom, but that he was preaching a crucified Lord: "to the Jews an obstacle that they cannot get over, to the pagans, madness, but to those who have been called, whether they are Jews or Greeks, a Christ who is the power and the wisdom of God. For God's foolishness is wiser than human wisdom, and God's weakness is stronger than human strength" (1 Cor 1:23-25).

Our Nobility

ST. IRENAEUS in the 2nd century wrote a succinct summary of God's plan in Christ Jesus for us: "God," he wrote, "became man in order that men might become God." Jesus came, not merely to teach us the way to share in God's divinity, but to *become* the way as He Himself underwent temptations and struggles and ultimately saw His human nature totally divinized after His passion and death in the glory of the resurrection: "Because of this, God highly exalted him and bestowed on him the name above every other name, so that at Jesus' name every knee must bend in the heavens, on the earth and under the earth, and every tongue proclaim to the glory of God the Father: Jesus Christ is Lord!" (Ph 2:9-11). By faith in His resurrection we have been empowered to live according to His love and truth. We are now able to "put on the mind of Christ" and become Christ-conscious.

Reborn from above by His Spirit (Jn 3:3, 5), our unspiritual or "carnal" minds are transformed, made capable of a spiritual way of thinking. "Your interests, however, are not in the unspiritual, but in the spiritual, since the Spirit of God has made his home in you" (Rm 8:9). Our spirit and God's indwelling Spirit "bear united witness (to the fact that) we are children of God" (Rm 8:16). This makes us heirs of God and co-heirs with Christ.

Silence creates the atmosphere in which we can put on the mind of Christ. One of the most important effects of putting on the mind of Christ in this inner silence — or inward stillness as Longfellow preferred to call it — is obedience to the will of God:

> Let us, then, labor for an inward stillness —
> An inward stillness and an inward healing;
> That perfect silence where the lips and heart
> Are still, and we no longer entertain
> Our own imperfect thoughts and vain opinions,
> But God alone speaks in us, and we wait
> In singleness of heart, that we may know
> His will, and in silence of our spirits,
> That we may do His will, and do that only.

St. Maximus the Confessor of the 7th century describes our becoming Christ-minded as part of the process of divinization, a kind of *symbiosis* whereby, becoming one with Christ, we overcome the world and help to reconcile it to God by bringing its diverse elements into one under His headship:

> *Then man makes one earth by uniting paradise with his inhabited world through chaste conversation. His united world then becomes no longer distinct by reason of the diversity of so many parts, but rather it is brought together into a synthesis so that man no longer suffers proliferation into separated parts. Then heaven and earth are united through a virtuous life similar to that of angels. Man no longer is bound down by his bodily condition but rises through an elevation of his soul to the invisible presence of God. He thus is able to make his own way by discerning what is prior and then go back to the material creation, to the things that are secondary.*
>
> *Then man unites the things known to his intellect and those known to his senses through a knowledge similar to that of the angels who see all of creation, not as separated into known and unknown, but man, become like to angels, is able to know by a knowledge that is the greatest infusion of true wisdom and given only to the worthy to know the difficult and the ineffable. Thus uniting created nature with the Uncreated through charity (a new and wonderful thing wrought in us through divine condescension) man shows all as one and the same through the power of grace. He sees all things in God, first as flowing from God into existence and secondly through them, rising to God as to the end of all moved creatures and the fixed and stable ground of their being, Who is the end of every rule and law, the end of every word and mind and of every nature, the infinite and unbound goal of all beings* (Ambigua).

Inward Stillness

IN THE PRECEDING CHAPTERS we examined various aspects of silence. We used silence to describe the perfect harmony of life within the Trinity. We tried to show that as whole persons made up of body, soul and spirit, we need silence on all these levels if we are to live in harmony with God's creative Word. Here we want to see, finally, how silence makes possible the fullest possible relationship we could have on earth with the indwelling risen Christ. Inner silence teaches us through the Spirit that in each of us is a *Center*. It is not a physical place, but rather a point of contact between our human consciousness and the consciousness of Jesus Christ. This point of contact is where we become one with Christ in love. And this union in love enables us to share our humanity with His, our true self with His true Self, making us by grace one with the Trinity and temples of the Godhead. The Trinity's infinite power is now available to us. No evil can prevail over us for we are all conquerers through this power of God which comes to us through the Incarnate Word, the risen Christ. "You have already overcome these false prophets, because you are from God and *you have in you One who is greater than anyone in this world"* (1 Jn 4:4). What was once impossible to us now is made possible by God's power operating within and around us. Silence creates the atmosphere in which we find it easier to surrender to God's power in humility and faith.

The Carnal Versus The Spiritual Mind

THAT DOES NOT mean there is no struggle. St. Paul speaks clearly to this point in his letter to the Romans. We reap what we sow. If our minds think evil thoughts we end up doing evil deeds. St. Paul knew that one who has such a "carnal," unspiritual mind cuts himself off from God's Spirit. "When self-indulgence is at work, the results are obvious: fornication, gross indecency and sexual irresponsibility; idolatry and sorcery; feuds and wrangling, jealousy, bad temper and quarrels; disagreements, factions, envy; drunkenness, or-

gies and similar things" (Gal 5:19-20). Jesus told us that to be
rid of these things we must cleanse the vessel from within as
it were, for out of a person's heart come all these evils which
render one unclean: "From the heart come evil intentions:
murder, adultery, fornication, theft, slander, etc." (Mt
15:18-20). He urges us to store up treasure in heaven (a
treasure of good deeds done in love), "for where your treasure is there your heart will likewise be" (Lk 12:14). He
speaks of the need for patience in our struggle. A tree does
not produce fruit overnight; the seed in the ground grows
imperceptibly (Mk 4:27).

The secret lies in our docility to the Spirit. Where there is
the Spirit, there is growth, there is love. Where there is the
Spirit, there is true liberty (2 Cor 3:18). Through the Spirit,
we live on a different level of awareness. We are given a
spiritual wisdom that allows us to grasp "the love of Christ
which is beyond all understanding" (Ep 3:19). We begin to
live by a whole new system of values. By constant inner
vigilance we make our own the values of Jesus. We make no
rash judgments for the Lord exhorts us not to "keep judging
according to appearances; let your judgment be according
to what is right" (Jn 7:24). It is only in inner stillness that we
can make right judgments, because it is in inner stillness that
we are able to sort out the voice of God from that of men.
This is the way Jesus lived. "As I hear, I judge, and my
judgment is just" (Jn 5:30). The Father is the Source of truth
and He has committed all judgment to the Son and has
given Him the authority to execute judgment also (Jn 5:22,
27). Peter was rebuked by the Lord because he wasn't listening to the voice of God within. "Get out of my sight, you
satan! You are not judging by God's standards but by man's"
(Mt 16:23). If we are not to make the same mistake, our
constant attitude must be that of young Samuel: "Speak,
Lord, your servant is listening" (1 Sam 3:10). Then will we

find harmony and peace and the desire to surrender passionately to God's Word.

Blessed Are The Poor In Spirit

THE LAW was built on justice. We read: "The Law was given by Moses but grace and truth by Christ Jesus" (Jn 1:17). Thus does St. John the Evangelist preface his proclamation of the Good News. Jesus brings with Him a new enlightenment and style of life free from all extrinsic laws as ends in themselves or as ultimate standards (Jn 8:35).

In His Sermon on the Mount Jesus lifted the basic beliefs of Judaism to a new level. He taught us that the Father truly loves us (Jn 16:27); that it is more gracious to give than to receive; that it is not the Heavenly Father who punishes His children for evil done, but that it is we who bring judgment upon ourselves. In the fifth chapter of St. Matthew's Gospel where we find the fullest account of the Sermon on the Mount, Jesus contrasts the Mosaic Law with His own new covenant and proclaims the poor, the meek, and the sorrowing blessed.

> *How happy are the poor in spirit;*
> *theirs is the kingdom of heaven.*
> *Happy the gentle:*
> *they shall have the earth for their heritage.*
> *Happy are those who mourn:*
> *they shall be comforted.*
> *Happy those who hunger and thirst for what is right:*
> *they shall be satisfied.*
> *Happy the merciful:*
> *they shall have mercy shown them.*
> *Happy the pure of heart:*
> *they shall see God.*

Happy the peacemakers:
   they shall be called sons of God.
Happy those who are persecuted in the cause of right:
   theirs is the Kingdom of heaven (Mt 5:3-10).

In silence we ultimately find the poverty of spirit that
each of us needs in order to grow spiritually. Poverty of
spirit is a call to constant conversion. It is best described in
biblical language as our exodus in complete dependence on
the Lord from our slavery to selfishness, sin and Satan and
our "passing over" to the promised land of freedom as
adopted children of God and heirs of the Kingdom of
Heaven. What seems to be poverty is really inner richness.
Those reborn of the Spirit, who have put on the mind of
Christ, will be happy when people abuse them and persecute them for His name. They will be able to turn the
other cheek when an enemy smites them on one. They will
not resist violence with violence. Each will seek reconciliation with his or her brother or sister and hold no grudges. As
they forgive each other, so the Father will forgive them. It is
no longer a matter of sinning. It's a matter of becoming
"perfected, even as your heavenly Father is perfect" (Mt
5:48). If a person takes your tunic, let him have your cloak as
well. If anyone asks you to go one mile, go with him two.
Give to anyone who asks, and if anyone wants to borrow, do
not turn away. Love your enemies and those who do you
wrong.

   In these ringing statements, Jesus contrasts the old Law
with the new standard demanded of His disciples: "You
have learnt how it was said . . . but I say this to you." It is
utterly impossible to live His way solely by human power.
Our strength must come from God. Entrance into the Kingdom of Heaven is measured by how we respond to the good
and react to the evil within and around us. A new conscious-

ness of our oneness in love with all God's creatures, especially our fellow human beings, is now very real to us.

If we are to measure our holiness or our life in Christ by our love for God and neighbor, we soon experience that such constant love, that such habitual self-giving cannot happen unless we have first truly surrendered to the triune God who dwells within. "For anyone who is in Christ, there is a new creation; the old creation has gone, and now the new one is here. It is all God's work" (2 Cor 5:17-18). This experience of being loved by God at the deepest level of our consciousness gives us strength and inspires us to new heights of self-giving and creativity.

Christ Is Risen

IN THE DEATH of Jesus on the cross, God the Father thundered out His everlasting *NO!* to sin and death. He smilingly whispered at the same time His *YES!!* to the new age. In Jesus the *Last Day* that could never be held within the broken limitations of earthly space and time had dawned and would never see a setting. The resurrection of Christ is a new beginning which brings to an end the domination of Satan in time and space. And yet, because His resurrection took place within the ambit of earthly time and space, the Lord has now somehow mysteriously entered into the history of our fallen humanity and from within is setting about to complete the eradication of sin, corruption and death, beginning in the hearts of His disciples. They are to be His leaven within humanity, the salt of the earth, the light of the world.

The resurrection breaks into history with the power of another world, God's world. It is not unlike a new creation, a return to the Garden of Eden wherein God walked and talked familiarly with man. In the resurrection, all of God's creative power became completely concentrated in the person of Jesus, thus raising Him from the dead. St. Paul writes, "He was crucified through weakness, yet He lives by the power of God" (2 Cor 13:4). God endowed the humanity of Jesus with the fullness of His power and glory. And Jesus "was established Son of God in power by the resurrection of the dead" (Rm 1:4).

Because Jesus possesses in His humanity the fullness of the Father's Spirit, all of us can now receive of His fullness. Jesus, by His resurrection is the "Prince of Life" (Ac 3:15). He is the cause, the origin, the center and the goal of the entire universe. He is indeed the Way, the Truth and the Life (Jn 14:6). Now risen from the dead, He makes it possible for us to share in His resurrection. He lives in us. Through His Spirit we come to know what our intellects alone could never have told us in a convincing way, viz. that God lives within us with all His power. He shares His life and power with us to the extent that we surrender ourselves in silent, loving abandonment to His living Word. Then He sends us forth as His ambassadors to bring His reconciliation to this shattered world (2 Cor 5:17-20).

Transformation

AMID THE FILTH AND SQUALOR of a broken and sordid world, we see the risen Lord breaking in to bring us His healing love and a share in His everlasting life. The power of the risen Lord who holds the keys of death and the underworld (Rv 1:17-18) lives within you and me. Therefore we already breathe the paschal victory of Christ even though we find ourselves surrounded still by the powers of darkness. We live in joyful hope for "nothing that exists, nothing still to come . . . can ever come between us and the love of God made visible in Christ Jesus our Lord" (Rm 8:39). The world

no longer has any power over us. Having experienced the
healing love of the risen Jesus, we are now empowered to
take our broken moment in the history of the human race
and our place in that disjointed chronicle and transform
them into a "new earth." Time and space may hold us in
their grasp, but we know that we live in Christ and, therefore, even now we live forever. St. Paul tells us how we are to
do it:

> *Since you have been brought back to life with Christ, you must look
> for the things that are in heaven, where Christ is, sitting at God's
> right hand. Let your thoughts be on heavenly things, not on the
> things that are on the earth because you have died, and now the life
> you have is hidden with Christ in God. But when Christ is revealed
> — and He is your life — you too will be revealed in all your glory
> with Him (Col 3:1-4).*

CHAPTER TEN

Silence To Hear
The Cries Of The Poor

WE HAVE PRESENTED in this book various aspects of silence.
We have seen how silence is the language of love, both
within the trinitarian community and in prayerful surrender to God and to our loved ones. It is the sign of how
integrated through God's healing love we have become on
the physical, psychic and spiritual levels.

There is a silence that comes when a child moves into
adolescence and begins to transcend the body's need for
sense gratification. There is the silence of the adolescent
who moves to greater thoughtfulness toward others in self-
sacrificing love, away from ego demands. There is the ongoing silence of the Christian adult who, guided by the Holy
Spirit and empowered by the Spirit's gifts, strives in
thought, word and deed to "hunger and thirst always for
what is right" (Mt 5:6).

Silence is both a sign of the healing effected by God's
Spirit in our prayer and an index of our transformation in
Christ. If our focus of attention turns away from ourselves
and centers upon the physical, psychological and spiritual

needs of others through loving service, we can say we are becoming true disciples of the Lord.

A New Christian View?

MANY CHRISTIANS are aware of a need to break through an understanding of Christianity that centered primarily on a vertical relationship between the individual Christian and God or, at most, as a part of a family or religious community. Catholics have been called by the teachings of Vatican II to move out into the horizontal dimension, not only to bring Christ into the market place but to release His risen presence that has always been there, especially among the poor, the oppressed and the suffering.

In their public documents against abortion, nuclear destructive over-kill and economic injustice, the American Catholic Bishops have united in their protest against the "powers and principalities" of a worldly, un-Christian culture. Bishop James Malone, president of the National Conference of Catholic Bishops, in discussing the Bishops' pastoral letter on the economy, emphasized the need to build up a public opinion based on Gospel values to support justice for the poor. The wider population has to be informed of these needs for justice since "the moral quality of a society is judged, not by how it honors the powerful, but by how it respects the claims and needs of the powerless."

Is this a "new" vision of Christianity? Is this not, rather, the very essence of how Christ lived His earthly life and what He taught His disciples? How can we ever think of ourselves as "religious" and pleasing to God, holy and striving to become perfect as our Heavenly Father, if we do not concern ourselves with the needs of others less fortunate than we? St. James phrased it in this way:

> *Take the case, my brothers, of someone who has never done a single good act but claims that he has faith. Will that faith save him? If one of the brothers or one of thē sisters is in need of clothes and has not enough food to live on, and one of you says to them, 'I wish you well; keep yourself warm and eat plenty,' without giving them these bare necessities of life, then what good is that? Faith is like that: if good works do not go with it, it is quite dead. . . You surely know that Abraham our father was justified by his deed, because he offered his son Isaac on the altar. There you see it: faith and deeds were working together; his faith became perfect by what he did. . . You see now that it is by doing something good, and not only by believing, that a man is justified (Jm 2:14-24).*

Christ, The Liberator

WHEN GOD'S LOVE burst upon our darkened world, in the person of Jesus Christ, His ministry was one of announcing the Good News of the Kingdom of God come among us and of denouncing the evils that obstructed it. Jesus was a prophet of hope, who not only gave the message of a new creation, but who became the medium through whom this new creation would come about. He came to awaken all men and women from their sleep and to bring light to them in their darkness. This enlightenment brought with it an awareness, not only of the basic goodness of each and every human being, but of every human being's call to use their talents to create a new and better world transformed by God's love.

Jesus said during His inaugural sermon on the Kingdom of God in the synagogue of Nazareth that God had anointed Him "to announce good news to the poor, to proclaim release for prisoners and recovery of sight for the blind, to let the broken victims go free, to proclaim the year of the Lord's favor" (Lk 4:16-22; cf. Is 61:1-2).

The Jews were expecting the "Day of Yahweh" when the

decisive and final intervention in the history of mankind would take place. The oppressed would at last see justice done. God would visit His people and fulfill His promises. He would reign in the world and His Kingdom of peace, justice and brotherhood would appear in all its perfection. All the individual and collective, material and spiritual aspirations of mankind would be fulfilled. The world would become what God had always destined it to be. Christ would lead His people back to Eden.

God's revolution would be the revolution which would end all revolutions. His Kingdom would come not through the violence of the sword, but in the power of the Word and in gentleness of spirit. "There is no need to be afraid, little flock, for it has pleased your Father to give you the Kingdom" (Lk 12:32). This Kingdom would be the fulfillment of man's aspirations and the transformation or completion, the recapitulation and the reconciliation of the entire world in and through Christ and His members. The Kingdom would usher into existence a new freedom from every type of alienation and dishonesty. It would be a liberation from sin, division, hatred, suffering and death. This is being achieved even now to some extent, but its full reality will take place only in the "Day of Yahweh."

Jesus, The Suffering Servant

JESUS'S PUBLIC LIFE was totally at the service of His people. He came to set them free and to lead them into the joy and peace of sharing His sonship before the Heavenly Father. He was the freest of all human beings. We see Him in this role precisely because He united in a silent, harmonious whole all the characteristics that make up a unique human personality. In every situation He responded with the fullness of His being, with an intense awareness of his true

identity as the Son of the Father. "My Father goes on working, and so do I" (Jn 5:17). He knew that everything He did
came from His Father. He lived only to serve the Father by
doing His will at all times (Jn 15:9). Jesus revealed an inner
consciousness of His ultimate worth and meaning as a human being which derived from His complete dependence
on the Father: "The Son can do nothing by himself; He can
do only what he sees the Father doing: and whatever the
Father does, the Son does too" (Jn 5:19). He had silenced
any and all untoward movements of His heart. There was no
vanity or self-seeking in any of His words or actions. His
primal motivation was to serve (Mk 10:45).

A scene in the life of Jesus always brought home very
poignantly to me the scope of His coming on earth and His
invitation to us to imitate His example. That is the scene of
the washing of His disciples' feet at the Last Supper. He put
aside His flowing, white outer garment, a sign to the Jews of
His teaching authority. He girded Himself around the waist
with a simple towel, the sign of a servant. Then He washed
their feet. When He had finished, He asked them: "Do you
understand what I have done to you? You call me Master
and Lord, and rightly; so I am. If I, then, the Lord and
Master, have washed your feet, you should wash each
others' feet. I have given you an example so that you may
copy what I have done to you. I tell you most solemnly, no
servant is greater than his master, no messenger is greater
than the man who sent him" (Jn 13:13-16).

Jesus fulfilled the prophecies of Isaiah, Jeremiah and
Hosea which related to the poor and the outcast of society,
the Amharez, the despised "people of the land" of the Old
Testament. His mission as Messiah was foretold by Isaiah:
"He has sent me to bring good news to the poor, to bind up
hearts that are broken; to proclaim liberty to captives, freedom to those in prison, to proclaim a year of favor from

Yahweh, a day of vengeance for our God, to comfort all
those who mourn, and to give for ashes a garland; for a
mourning robe the oil of gladness, for despondency, praise"
(Is 61:1-3).

Jeremiah characterizes the holy man as one who knows
God and serves the poor. "Your father ate and drank like
you, but he practiced honesty and integrity, so all went well
for him. He used to examine the cases of poor and needy,
then all went well. Is not that what it means to know me? — it
is Yahweh who speaks" (Jr 22:15-16). God does not want
rituals and laws, sacrifices and formalized prayers. God
wants justice, love and peace. In this vein, Isaiah captures
what it means to please God and win His favor through
service to the poor and downtrodden:

What are your endless sacrifices to me?
I am sick of holocausts of rams
and the fat of calves. . .
When you stretch out your hands
I turn my eyes away.
You may multiply your prayers,
I shall not listen.
Your hands are covered with blood,
Wash, make yourselves clean. . .
Cease to do evil.
Learn to do good,
search for justice,
help the oppressed,
be just to the orphan,
plead for the widow (Is 1:11-17).

So Jesus turned upon the religious of His day, the
Pharisees and the Scribes, and judged them severely for
their hypocrisy and their vanity. He especially denounced
them for imposing heavy burdens upon the poor. The

whole 23rd chapter of St. Matthew's Gospel is Christ's indictment of the ruling, religious class who were so caught up in all forms of legalism, casuistry and hypocrisy, that they had lost sight of the true meaning of religion. He condemned those leaders who used religion for their own selfish interests. He came to set people free from the externals of the Law in order that through His Spirit they could live more fully that for which the Law was intended, namely, love. St. Paul understood this well when he wrote: "If you are led by the Spirit, no law can touch you" (Gal 5:18).

The Early Christians

WHEN JESUS' EARLY DISCIPLES received the outpouring of His Spirit, they began to love each other and to share all they had in common. "The whole group of believers was united, heart and soul; no one claimed for his own use anything that he had, as everything they owned was held in common" (Ac 4:12). Pagans were converted to Christianity, not through the arguments of the first Christians, but by their example of love for one another. These early Christians knew that only by assuming full responsibility for their world, their lives and the lives of others, would they know God in Christ Jesus and be welcome in His Kingdom.

Following the example of St. Paul, the early Fathers of the Church focused on a deep concern for the poor, the suffering and the afflicted. They had experienced the infinite love of God in Jesus and this humbled them and gave them a spirit of poverty that drove them to serve the poor with heartfelt compassion and mercy. They recognized different degrees of poverty and oppression, the most evident being that of physical need: hunger, thirst, nakedness, sickness, imprisonment, etc. (cf. Mt 25:35-40). With St. James, they knew that faith without good works was dead

(Jm 2:15-17). St. Basil of the 4th century speaks of a "common and universal sharing of possessions. It is lawful for each one," he wrote, "to take from these common possessions to the degree that he is able and that is suited to his needs" (*Homily* 12, 4). All persons were considered to have a strict right to the use of what they needed in order to live decently. Those who possessed more talents and wealth felt the need to share these with the others, that they were merely God's administrators of a common good given them by God to be shared with those less fortunate than they. St. Ambrose described the situation as it was mutually perceived by Eastern and Western Christians of the early Church in these words:

> *The Lord our God willed that his earth should be the common property of all mankind, and so He offered its produce for all to enjoy; but man's avarice distributed the right of its possession* (Exposition of Ps 118, 8th Sermon).

He went on to say that one cannot justify the possession of great wealth by appealing to a poverty of detachment that lies only in the "spirit" and never quite condescends to become a true detachment in fact. Again we see from the early Fathers that this sharing of one's wealth with the poor is not a generous condescension on the part of the wealthy but it flows from the spiritual insight that the poor have a *right* to it in justice since all things belong to God, the Father of us all. If, as the Fathers claim, wealth has no other purpose than to be used for the common good, it follows that distinctions between rich and poor should gradually diminish.

You Are
To Be Christ To The World Today

> *Go out to the whole world; proclaim the Good News to all creation.*
> *. . . these are the signs that will be associated with believers: in my*
> *name they will cast out devils; they will have the gift of tongues; they*
> *will pick up snakes in their hands and be unharmed should they*
> *drink deadly poison; they will lay their hands on the sick, who will*
> *recover (Mk 16:16-18).*

This was the Lord's commission to His first disciples. It is His commission to us today. It is a call to serve the poor. Pope Paul VI, in his Apostolic Exhortation on the *Evangelical Witness of Religious Life*, renews the pleas of Jesus on behalf of the very poor in our midst today: "From their personal distress and collective misery, you hear 'the cry of the poor' rising up more pressing than ever. Was it not in order to respond to their appeal as God's privileged ones that Christ came, even going so far as to identify Himself with them?. . . In a world experiencing a greater degree of development, this persistence of poverty-stricken multitudes and individuals constitutes a pressing call for a 'change in everybody's thinking and habits,' especially for you who follow Christ more closely in this condition of self-emptying."

The Cry
Of The Poor Echoed In Our Own Lives

POPE PAUL VI gives us two ways by which we can identify with God's suffering and compassion for the poor of the world. First of all, he tells us that God is not neutral to injustice. Therefore, *we* can never be neutral or indifferent to any form of injustice on any level in the lives of individuals, families, communities or institutions. All of us are interrelated and interdependent. We must make our voices heard. We must speak out against the injustices inflicted upon the less fortunate, the weak and the vulnerable in our midst. To be silent in a cowardly way is to betray a sacred trust.

Secondly, he encourages us to hear in the cries of the poor a call for personal conversion. "It obliges you to a- waken consciences to the drama of misery and to the de- mands of social justice made by the Gospel and the Church." Awakening of consciences comes once our own consciences have been stung by the many injustices we see perpetrated on our brothers and sisters, wherever they may live, of whatever faith or nationality, sex or age. We can only con- vert other individuals, groups and institutional in- frastructures to God's ways if we ourselves have been con- verted. We can be effectively engaged in alleviating such injustices and sufferings to the degree that we have actively removed such injustices in our own individual dealings with others.

Prayer And Ministry

HERE WHAT has been said in earlier chapters reinforces our thesis that, as we pray, so we live. Out of the silence of our surrendering love for God in which we experience the Lord's compassion for the world, we are moved to do what we can to alleviate injustice. No pope or bishop, preacher or writer can outline how you or I should act "justly" amidst the anguish and sufferings of our brothers and sisters. It is in prayer that we allow the anguished cry of the poor for justice to make itself heard in the depths of our being. And as we struggle with the significance of their cry for us, we realize that their lot is indeed our own, their suffering is also ours.

What affects them must affect us deeply. The bell tolls for each of us as it tolls for each of them.

Pity alone, though, is worthless. Faith without good works is dead! Wherever our sympathy leads us, we must go too if possible. We are called to *live* the Gospel not merely to preach it. We are impelled by the inner presence of God to enter the political, social and economic arenas and there to become prophetic witnesses to His ideal of justice, brotherhood and universal peace.

How we do so will depend greatly on our talents and state of life. We cannot all witness to and bring about the reign of God in the same way or with the same talents as Martin Luther King, Jr. or Mother Teresa of Calcutta or Archbishop Oscar Romero in El Salvador have done. But each of us should respond according to our own talents, charisms, place and time in the Body of Christ. A housewife will fight injustices in her family, community and world arenas differently from the way a priest or a law-maker will. Yet all of us must move continually in wider circles toward the larger community where love grows as we freely assume responsibility for the happiness of our brothers and sisters, whoever and wherever they may be.

A Reconciler

PRAYER AND MINISTRY go together. There can never be any separation. True prayer always leads to a transformation that is witnessed by deeds. In prayer we become more aware that we are called in every life situation to be instruments of unity (Jn 17:23), reconcilers of those who live in disharmony (2 Cor 5:18), and ambassadors of peace (1 Th 5:13).

We will find ourselves seeking to become leaven actively reforming, according to our individual talents and opportunities, the unjust societal structures that impede the liberation of others who are being denied the possibility of living up to their God-given potential. Jesus in His role as prophet challenged the Jewish religio-political establishment to seek the path of reconciliation. In a similar way you and I are called by Him to challenge society today to grant freer access to God's gifts and resources so that all might more fully enjoy them and come to experience God as a loving and benevolent Father.

The Paschal Victory

THE CHURCH has always been aware of the role its members were to play in eradicating the root causes of injustice, economic, social or political. Its leaders have an especially important part to play in this regard as, in their efforts at evangelization, they work for human development and the extension of the Kingdom of God here on earth. The American Bishops in their pastoral letter on the economy remind us all as individuals of our personal responsibility to be the servants of the poor, the sick and the marginalized of our world. "Lay men and women in a wide array of vocations have great opportunities to carry out this mission, which belongs to every member of the Christian community. We know many of them — teachers, homemakers, laborers, lawyers, politicians and numerous others — who have used their skills and their compassion to seek innovative ways to carry out the goals we are proposing in this letter" (#150). To preach the Gospel of Jesus without showing His concern in a concrete practical way on the economic, social, cultural and political levels is to fail to be doers of the Word rather than mere listeners thereof.

Call To Decision

GOD'S KINGDOM here on earth will come about only with our human cooperation and within the context of our human situation. The building up of this Kingdom challenges us everyday of our lives. It challenges our attitudes and our way of doing things. It calls us to make decisions in the here and now. In the words of George Mangatt:

> *The kingdom of God Jesus proclaimed is not a purely other-worldly reality to be realized only in the future, but something that has effectively entered into human history, transforming the whole of human existence. It does not consist merely in the salvation of the soul, but in the total liberation of the human person from all forms of slavery and affliction, spiritual, material and social. It is God's fatherly rule of mercy, forgiveness, justice and universal love. Where there is any form of slavery, injustice, hatred or opposition there God cannot be ruling, there the Kingdom of God cannot exist. The total human situation — individual, social, economic, political — is assumed into God's rule and Kingdom; where anti-God forces in any form dominate and oppress God's children, God's rule cannot be real. That is why Jesus conceived his mission as an integral liberation of the whole human person; that is why he went about healing the sick, feeding the hungry, freeing the possessed; that is why he fought the injustices of the Jewish aristocracy* ("Jesus and Service," *pp. 276-277*).

The process began with Jesus, but the total liberation of the human race from every form of slavery and affliction — spiritual, material and social — is a process that continues in and through each one of us in cooperation with the Holy Spirit in faith, hope and love. Our first response lies in the area of becoming informed about the injustices that exist in the lives of individuals, communities and nations. We need to become convinced that each of us is important, a vital link in the chain of social progress, and that we are all interdependent and interconnected. Before we can even think of what to do to bring resources to persons deprived of them, we need to be in touch with the actual situation of poverty and oppression in our local, national and international scenes.

Complexity And Challenge

FOR EXAMPLE, are you aware that 800 million people in the countries of the Third World live in conditions of absolute destitution which, in Robert McNamara's definition, is a condition of life so limited by malnutrition, illiteracy, disease, high infant mortality and low life expectancy as to be beneath any national definition of human decency? Half of the world's population, 2.26 billion people, live in countries where the per capita annual income is the equivalent of $400 or less whereas in the United States the per capita income is $12,530. Some 450 million people are under-nourished or facing starvation, despite abundant harvests in America and Europe. Fifteen out of every 100 children born in the countries of the Third World will die before the age of five and hundreds of thousands of those who survive will be stunted physically and/or mentally. The average life expectancy of such people (except for China) is 48 years while in the USA it is 74 (Cf. *Overseas Development Council: U.S. Policy and the Third World: Agenda 1983*).

We need to know how multinational institutions operate, both in our own country and abroad, especially in the underdeveloped nations of the world, how they often obstruct justice and promote conditions that lead to greater poverty, illiteracy, sickness, hunger and malnutrition. The power of such corporations is enormous, second only to the power of affluent countries such as the United States. They literally control the lives of billions of people and subject them to an ever increasing level of inhuman existence. Nothing short of a conversion, a change of heart from top to bottom and a corresponding change in the way we do business, will suffice if justice is ever to prevail.

The Synod of Bishops meeting in Rome in 1971 issued the following statement in union with the Holy Father: "In the face of the present-day world situation, marked by the grave sin of injustice, we recognize our responsibility and our inability to overcome it by our own strength. . . Such a situation urges us to listen with a humble and open heart to the word of God, as he shows us new paths toward action on behalf of justice in the world" (*The Pope Speaks*, p. 381).

What To Do?

IN THAT SYNOD, the Bishops with the Pope humbly confessed their powerlessness before the enormity of such social problems. So we are faced with the need to pray and then to act. Prayer that does not lead us to do what we can is not true Christian prayer. In this there is, of course, a necessary tension. We find God's peace and joy in prayer but trial and tribulation in the world. It's like the cross which our Lord faced squarely after His colloquy with the Father in the Garden of Gethsemane. In prayer we find the strength we need to face our problems squarely. In consultation with others and as part of concerned activist groups, we will find that we can do much in the way of alleviating many conditions where inequality and loss of human dignity currently prevail. At times our involvement may take the form of a protest, active demonstrations, letter writing campaigns, raising money, collecting food, clothing and medicine, or witnessing to pro-life principles and against the evils of abortion and euthanasia. When we sincerely desire to make "an option for the poor," we must believe that God will honor that option for we are responding in fact to the name by which He calls us.

As Jesus suffered for doing good and even went to His ignominious death on the cross in part because of his outspoken stand against the established powers of His day and in favor of the poor and the suffering of body, soul and spirit, so He promises all of us that we will also share in His sufferings and the cross and become a sign of contradiction in opposition to the powers of evil in families, institutions, towns and countries, yes, even in the world in which we live today. The cross is the permanent sign or symbol in our lives that we are being faithful to the Word we daily hear in the integrating silence of our prayer. As we go forth in the same silence, we continue to listen to the Word who speaks to us through His Spirit, giving us the wisdom to discern what we should do concretely in our daily involvement on behalf of the poor.

Before we bring our gift to the Eucharistic table, we must bring reconciliation and peace to those who are still at odds with one another. We see how ministry leads to prayer and prayer to ministry as we live out the Exodus passover in the details of our daily service to the needy of this world. By doing works of justice and mercy we become bread that is broken and shared. Religion without a sense of social responsibility is magic and not religion. Receiving the Body of Christ without receiving His members has to be some kind of sacrilege. Believing in God and the Good News that His Son has brought us without visiting the sick, the poor, those imprisoned, giving food and drink to the hungry and thirsty is to have totally failed to understand the Gospel message (Mt 25:31-41).

Silence And Speech

THUS WE COME to the end which was our beginning. Only in the silence of our hearts can we hear the Good News and be healed of our sinfulness and brokenness by God's outpoured love in Christ Jesus and His Spirit. Such silence leads us to greater openness to Christ and the promptings of His Spirit in the context of our daily life and ministry. True silence is the atmosphere in which love grows. But silence is only effective to the degree that it produces much fruit.

We are called to become God's Word, spoken to others who cannot hear that Word *unless* we speak It, softly and clearly in our daily lives. Silence is good only if it leads us to communicate the Word with which we have been in communion. That Word is Jesus Christ, the Speech of God, who in the silence of love and the integration of Himself, body, soul and spirit, gave Himself to the poor of this world that they might have life and have it more abundantly (Jn 10:10). He gives us the privilege of carrying His healing Word to the broken and downhearted. We will be God's Word, spoken again in a noisy world, to the degree that we have first been silent in body, soul and spirit and let His Word take root in the very depth of our hearts. Then we will go forth to obey and communicate the Word that we heard in silence by our involvement in redressing the grievances and injustices around us. Prayer and ministry go together. Listening in obedience to God's Word goes together with our speaking God's truth in love. Silence, communication and communion cannot be separated in the Body of Christ.

Eternal life is this: to know the only true God and Him whom He has sent, Jesus Christ (Jn 17:3). To know Him is to love Him. We love Him when we recognize and serve Him in one another. For we all belong to Christ and He belongs to God. Whatever we do for each other in love, we truly do for Him.

This has taught us love —
that he gave up his life for us;
and we, too, ought to give up our lives for our brothers.

If a man who was rich enough in this world's goods
saw that one of his brothers was in need,
but closed his heart to him,
how could the love of God be living in him?
My children,
our love is not to be just words or mere talk,
but something real and active;
only by this can we be certain
that we are children of the truth
and be able to quieten our conscience in his presence,
whatever accusations it may raise against us,
because God is greater than our conscience and he knows everything
. . . His commandments are these:

that we believe in the name of His Son Jesus Christ
and that we love one another
as he told us to.

Whoever keeps his commandments
lives in God and God lives in him.

We know that he lives in us
by the Spirit that he has given us (1 Jn 3:16-20, 23-24).

A Prayer Exercise
Of A Silent Heart

I WOULD LIKE to share with you an example of an integrating form of prayer of the heart which brings us into that inner silence of body, soul and spirit about which we have written in the preceding chapters. We must never get too tied up with the details of any one technique, but rather we should learn to adapt such things to our own prayer needs and test the effectiveness of the technique by the fruit produced. We realize that the Spirit does work through techniques, but the Spirit can also work immediately without any such "scaffolding." Experimentation should be tried to see what renders greater fruit.

In general we Westerners put too much stress on our intellectual and imaginational powers while ignoring our bodies and above all our spirits in prayer. It is important that we integrate these three. And thus we have to begin with the physical state of our body. The body is a tremendous field of chemical and electrical charges, interacting with the world around it. The environment in which we pray influences the body. It is imperative, therefore, that we begin to pray by starting to relax the body, bringing it into the "heart," into the highest possible concentration of all its faculties.

While it is true we can pray on a subway, the deepest type of prayer necessitates transcending our habitual activities. It requires a state of high anticipation, of silent waiting on the Lord, apart from all extraneous distractions. For this, choose a quiet place. The time is also important. I have found from my own personal experience that three hours or so of deep sleep can be a most effective way of preparing the body and mind for deeper prayer. The next best time is upon rising, before we do anything else in a busy day.

Choose the most relaxed position. For some this might be on a cushion in the lotus position. For others it might mean sitting on a straight chair. What is most important is that the spinal cord be straight up and down with no hunching of the shoulders. Breathing deeply is helpful if we are to enter into a oneness with the indwelling Trinity because it provides the oxygen we need for such a concentrated effort. It focuses our attention on something beyond our own often vagrant thoughts and lifts our minds to the contemplation of the Triune God who is beyond conceptualization. Breathing diaphragmatically also relieves much tension. You can know whether you are breathing diaphragmatically when you feel the muscles of your diaphragm move out as you inhale and in as you exhale.

Physical Silence

Now CLOSE your eyes. Continue to breathe rhythmically. Concentrate on each part of your body, starting with the top of the head, the forehead, the cheeks, the chin, the neck and shoulders. Command all tension to disappear. Think now of your chest area: heart, lungs and abdomen. Keep breathing deeply all the time. Relax even more as you lengthen your exhalation. Let go of any tightness in your arms, elbows, wrists, hands, fingers, hips, thighs, knees, calves, ankles and toes.

Remember, God is within you, sustaining you and protecting you at all times. Your body is His temple and His Spirit lives within you. Breathe deeply, filling your lungs with God's breath. Feel His energy course through your whole being. Reach up in loving adoration and surrender to the loving Father. Let go of the control that you exercise over your life. Shut out all extraneous and internal noises. Experience the love of God pulsating within you. Desire to love Him only in complete submission to His will.

Psychic Silence

ONCE YOUR BODY is relaxed, you can move on to the elements that make up your psyche, the faculties within you of imagination, emotions, memory, intellect and will. Seek to silence all of these in order to bring your spirit into a deeper oneness with the Spirit of the Lord.

Picture in your mind a building twenty stories tall. Imagine that you are on the top floor. The bell rings. The door opens and you walk in. You press the number 0 or Basement. Feel the elevator descend ever so slowly. Allow yourself to sink into an ever deeper state of relaxation as you pass each floor. Pause at each storey for a just a moment. Say to yourself: "19: I'm becoming more and more relaxed. 18: . . . going deeper into my true self. 17: It feels great! 16: I surrender myself to You, God, who are within me, loving me. 15: Take everything, O Lord. 14: . . . 13: . . . like a bird, gliding effortlessly in the sky. 12: . . . 11: I'm getting closer now to God. 9: I feel weightless, as if floating in the water. 8: . . . no worries; only silence. 7: Come, Lord Jesus. 6: I am getting deeper into myself.

5: . . . at each step I am going down deeper into a state of complete relaxation and greater inner silence. 4: I see a meadow brimming with spring flowers; the sun is shining; birds are singing. . . 3: God, it is good to be alive! 2: I see Christ as a candle burning in a deep cave without any flickering. Perfect tranquility. 1: And I am totally one with Him. 0: God opens His arms and enfolds me in His beautiful, soothing light and makes me light!"

Spirit Silence

NOW YOU WISH to empty yourself of all thoughts so that you can be filled with the formless presence of God — Father, Son and Spirit — the living Trinity that dwells within you. As you continue in a relaxed manner to breathe deeply in and out, synchronize your breathing with these two names who are unseen but very really present: Jesus . . . Abba.

Breathe in deeply and mentally recite the name and experience the presence of: *JESUS.* Breathe out slowly and mentally say the name and experience the presence of: *ABBA.* Continue to breathe in slowly and mentally think of Jesus. Breathe out slowly and mentally think: Abba. Jesus . . . Abba . . . Do not be concerned about any thought content. Let the words become for you a way to rivet your attention and focus your mind so that you can reach a meta-rational state of concentration that will allow you to listen in a deeply receptive mood to God as He speaks to you in the utter silence of your body, soul and spirit.

This is what it means to pray in the heart and in the spirit. It is to allow yourself to be filled like an empty receptacle with the Spirit's gifts of faith, hope and love. I believe this is what St. Paul was referring to when he told us that our recited prayers are not the highest form of adoration but that it is when we yield to the Spirit of Jesus and allow Him to pray within us that we pray the best. To pray with all our faculties, surrendering to the Heavenly Father in loving silence before the Lord, is to pray with hearts that are one with Jesus. It is to let His Spirit pray in our spirit — wordlessly and in loving silence. Silence becomes the milieu in which we pass our waking moments creatively listening to God's Word and surrendering to His will through the loving power of His divinizing Spirit.

> *The Spirit too helps us in our weakness, for we do not know how to pray as we ought; but the Spirit himself makes intercession for us with groanings which cannot be expressed in speech. He who searches hearts knows what the Spirit means, for the Spirit intercedes as God himself wills (Rm 8:26-27).*

Bibliography

Works cited or used in the writing, according to the chapters.

Chapter One_____

1. T.S. Eliot: *Complete Poems and Plays* (N.Y.: Harcourt, Brace & World Inc. 1952).
2. Soren Kierkegaard: *The Sickness unto Death*; tr. Walter Lowrie (Garden City, N.Y.: Doubleday, 1954).
3. Meister Eckhart: *Meister Eckhart*; tr. C. de B. Evans (London: John M. Watkins, 1958).
4. P.M. Bruno, OCSO: *Le Silence Monastique dans la Tradition Cisterciénne* (Besancon: L'Est, 1954).
5. Nietzsche: *The Portable Nietzsche* (N.Y.: Viking, 1954).
6. St. Hilary of Poitiers: *The Trinity*; tr. Stephen McKenna, C.SS.R., in *The Fathers of the Church Series*; Vol. 25 (Wash. D.C.: Catholic University Press, 1954; Bk. 2).
7. Richard of St. Victor: *De Trinitate*; Bk. III; *PL* 196.

Chapter Two_____

1. T.S. Eliot: *The Four Quartets* (N.Y.: Harcourt, Brace & World, Inc., 1943).
2. George Leonard: *The Silent Pulse* (N.Y.: Elsevier-Dutton Publishing Co. Inc., Bantam Books, 1978; preface).
3. Serge Bulgakov: "De Verbe Incarne," in: *La Sagesse Divine et la Théanthropie* (Paris, 1943).
4. Emil Brunner: *Man in Revolt* (Philadelphia, PA: Westminster Press 1976).

5. St. Ignatius to the Ephesians, *The Fathers of the Church Series*; Vol. 15 (Wash. D.C.: McGrath, 1946).
6. V.E. Frankl: *La psychothérapie et son image de l'homme* (Paris, 1970).
7. P.C. Hodgson: *Jesus-Word and Presence* (Philadelphia, PA: Fortress Press, 1971).
8. George A. Maloney, S.J.: *Man-The Divine Icon* (Pecos, N.M.: Dove Publications, 1973).
9. St. Augustine: *Confessions*, tr. F.J. Sheed (N.Y.: Sheed & Ward, 1968).
10. H. Lubienska de Lenval: *Le Silence a l'ombre de la Parole* (Paris: Casterman, 1965) in: *Bible et Vie Chretienne Series*.
11. George A. Maloney, S.J.: *Centering on the Lord Jesus; The Whole Person at Prayer* (Wilmington, DE: M. Glazier, Inc., 1982).

Chapter Three

1. Thomas Merton: *Contemplative Prayer* (Garden City, N.Y.: Doubleday, 1970).
2. Blaise Pascal: *Pénsées*; tr. W.F. Trotter (N.Y.: Random House, 1940).
3. George A. Maloney, S.J.: *Listen, Prophets!* (Denville, N.J.: Dimension Books, 1975).
4. Romano Guardini: *Living God* (N.Y.: Sheed & Ward, 1967).
5. Karl Rahner: *Everyday Faith* (N.Y.: Sheed & Ward, 1972).
6. Max Picard: *The World of Silence* (Chicago: H. Regnery Co., 1952).
7. Paul Tournier: *The Whole Person in a Broken World*; tr. by John & Helen Doberstein (N.Y.: Harper & Row, 1964).

Chapter Four

1. Charles Cummings, OCSO: *Spirituality and the Desert Experience* (Denville, N.J.; Dimension Books, 1978).
2. C. de Hueck Doherty: *Poustinia* (Notre Dame: Ave Maria Press, 1974).

3. Elizabeth O'Connor: *Search for Silence* (Waco, TX: Word Books, 1972).
4. Emma Jung & Maria-Louise von Franz: *The Grail Legend* (N.Y.: G.P. Putnam's Sons, 1963).
5. Dr. Rollo May: *Man's Search for Himself* (N.Y.: W.W. Norton & Co., 1953).
6. George A. Maloney, S.J.: *Pilgrimage of the Heart. A Treasury of Eastern Christian Spirituality* (San Francisco: Harper & Row, 1983).
7. George A. Maloney, S.J.: *Prayer of the Heart* (Notre Dame, IN: Ave Maria Press, 1981).
8. Helen Waddell: *The Desert Fathers* (Ann Arbor: The Univ. of Michigan Press, 1957).
9. St. John Climacus: *Ladder of Divine Ascent*; tr. Colm Luibheid N. Russell (N.Y.: Paulist Press, 1982).
10. Thomas Merton: *The Climate of Monastic Prayer* (Spencer, MA: Cistercian Publications, 1968).
11. *Imitation of Christ* (Hollywood, CA: Marcel Rodd, 1945).
12. George A. Maloney, S.J.: *Death, Where is Your Sting?* (Staten Island: Alba House, 1984).
13. St. John of the Cross: *The Collected Works of Saint John of the Cross*; tr. Kieran Kavanaugh & Otilio Rodriguez (Wash. D.C: Institute of Carmelite Studies Publ., 1973).
14. St. Gregory of Nyssa: *Homily on the Canticle of Canticles*, in: *Patrologia Graeca* (PG) Vol. 44.
15. St. Maximus the Confessor: *Ambigua*: *PG* 91.
16. Teilhard de Chardin: *The Phenomenon of Man*; tr. Bernard Wall (N.Y.: Harper Torchbooks, 1959).

Chapter Five

1. Manuel Gonzalez Garcia: *Jesus Silent*; tr. Sr. M. Monica (N.Y.: P.J. Kenedy, 1937).
2. George A. Maloney, S.J.: *Bright Darkness* (Denville, N.J.: Dimension Books, 1977).
3. G.M. Hopkins, S.J.: *Poems*; ed. N.H. Mackenzie (London: The Folio Society, 1974).

4. George A. Maloney, S.J.: *Broken But Loved* (Staten Island, N.Y.: Alba House, 1982).
5. John A. Sanford: *The Invisible Partners* (N.Y.: Paulist Press, 1980).
6. Geoffrey Hoyland: *The Use of Silence* (London: SPCK, 1955).
7. Joachim Jeremias: *Prayers of Jesus*, tr. Christoph Burchard (London: SCM Press, 1967).
8. Jurgen Moltmann: *The Gospel of Liberation*; tr. H. Wayne Pipkin (Waco, TX: Word Books, 1973).
9. J. Moltmann: *The Crucified God* (London: SCM Press, 1974).
10. St. Ignatius to the Ephesians, in *The Fathers of the Church Series*; Vol. 25 (Wash., D.C., 1946).

Chapter Six

1. Karl Rahner: *Mary Mother of the Lord* (N.Y.: Sheed & Ward, 1963).
2. George A. Maloney, S.J.: *Mary the Womb of God* (Denville, N.J.: Dimension Books, 1976).
3. J. Roche, S.J.: *Le Silence de la Vièrge* (Paris: P. Lethielleux, 1961).
4. *Vatican Council II: The Conciliar and Post Conciliar Documents*; ed. Walter M. Abbott, S.J. (N.Y.: Guild Press, America Press, Association Press, 1966).
5. George A. Maloney, S.J.: *Bright Darkness* (Denville, N.J.: Dimension Books, 1977).
6. E. Danniel and B. Olivier: *Woman is the Glory of Man* (Westminster, MD: Newman Press, 1966).
7. L. Beirnaert: *Mystique et continence* (Paris, 1952).
8. Hugo Rahner: *Our Lady-the Church* (Chicago, IL, 1965).
9. Louis Bouyer: *The Seat of Wisdom* (N.Y.: Sheed & Ward, 1960).
10. *Mariology*; ed. Juniper B. Carol (Milwaukee, WI, 1957).
11. Dr. Irene Claremont de Castillejo: *Knowing Woman* (Colophon, N.Y.: Harper, 1973).
12. St. John of the Cross: *The Collected Works*; op.cit.
13. T.S. Eliot: *Four Quartets*; op.cit.

14. E. Schillebeeckx, O.P.: *Mary Mother of the Redemption* (N.Y.: Sheed & Ward, 1964).

Chapter Seven

1. Michel Siffre: "Six Months Alone in a Cave," in: *National Geographic* (March, 1975; V. 147:3; pp. 426-435).
2. Gabriel Marcel: *The Mystery of Being*; tr. Réné Hague (Chicago: H. Regnery Co., 1960).
3. Eugene C. Kennedy: *A Time for Love* (Garden City, N.Y.: Doubleday & Co., 1970).
4. Rollo May: *Love and Will* (N.Y.: Dell Publishing Co., 1969).
5. C. Gallagher, G. Maloney, M. Rousseau, P. Wilczak: *Embodied in Love*; *Sacramental Spirituality and Sexual Intimacy* (N.Y.: Crossroad, 1983).
6. Jean Vanier: *Community and Growth* (N.Y.: Paulist Press, 1979).
7. Henri Nouwen: "Solitude & Community," in: *Worship* (Jan., 1978).
8. Martin Buber: *I and Thou* 2nd ed., tr. R.G. Smith (N.Y.: Scribner, 1958).
9. George A. Maloney, S.J.: *Nesting in the Rock* (Denville, N.J.: Dimension Books, 1977).
10. Teilhard de Chardin: *The Divine Milieu*; tr. B. Wall (London: Wm. Collins Sons & Co., 1960).
11. M. Buber: *I and Thou*; op.cit.
12. T.S. Eliot: *Four Quartets*; op.cit.
13. M.T. Kelsey: *Caring*; *How Can We Love One Another?* (N.Y.: Paulist Press, 1981).
14. Rollo May: *Love and Will*; op.cit.

Chapter Eight

1. Jacques Sarano: *The Meaning of the Body*; tr. James H. Farley (Philadelphia, PA: Westminster Press, 1966). Preface by Dr. Paul Tournier.

2. C.A. van Peursen: *Body, Soul, Spirit: A Survey of the Body-Mind Problem* (London: Oxford Univ. Press, 1966).

3. W.E. Oates: *Nurturing Silence in a Noisy Heart* (Garden City, N.Y.: Doubleday & Co., 1979).

4. George A. Maloney, S.J.: *Inscape: God at the Heart of Matter* (Denville, N.J.: Dimension Books, 1978).

5. Dr. Carl E. and LaVonne Braaten: *The Living Temple* (N.Y.: Harper & Row, 1967); tr. Melvin Cherno.

6. Carl G. Jung: *Modern Man in Search of a Soul* (N.Y.: Harcourt, Brace & World, 1933).

7. J.M. Dechanet: *Christian Yoga* (N.Y.: Harper & Row, 1972).

8. Eric W. Hayden: *Everyday Yoga for Christians* (Valley Forge, PA: Judson Press, 1972).

9. William Johnston, S.J.: *Christian Zen* (N.Y.: Harper & Row, 1971).

10. George A. Maloney, S.J.: *Prayer of the Heart* (Notre Dame, IN: Ave Maria Press, 1980).

11. St. John Climacus: *Ladder of Divine Ascent* (N.Y.: Paulist Press, 1982).

12. *The Shakers* (N.Y.: Paulist Press, 1983); ed. R.E. Whitson.

13. Jean-Jacques Latour: "Solitude et Liturgie," in: *Revue Christus* (Paris; Jan., 1966).

Chapter Nine

1. A. Hulsbosch: *God's Creation* (N.Y.: Sheed & Ward, 1965).

2. Karl Menninger: *Whatever Became of Sin?* (N.Y.: Hawthorn Books, Inc., 1973).

3. George A. Maloney, S.J.: *The Cosmic Christ* (N.Y.: Sheed & Ward, 1968).

4. A.D. Galloway: *The Cosmic Christ* (London: Nisbet, 1951).

5. L.H. Taylor: *The New Creation* (N.Y.: Pageant Press, 1958).

6. Lars Thunberg: *Microcosm and Mediator: The Theological Anthropology of Maximus the Confessor* (Copenhagen: Lund, 1965).

7. Christopher F. Mooney: *Teilhard de Chardin and the Mystery of Christ* (N.Y.: Harper & Row, 1966).

8. H.C. White, Jr., ed.: *Christians in a Technological Era* (N.Y.: Seabury, 1964).
9. *The Christian in the World: Readings in Theology.* Compiled at the Canianum, Innsbruck (N.Y.: Kenedy, 1965).

Chapter Ten

1. Text of the American Bishops *Pastoral Letter on the Economy* (Kansas City, MO: *NCR*, 1984).
2. George A. Maloney, S.J.: *Bright Darkness*, op.cit.
3. Raymond E. Brown: *Jesus God and Man* (Milwaukee, WI: Bruce, 1967).
4. Gerald Vann, O.P.: *The Pain of Christ and the Sorrow of God* (London: Blackfriars, 1947).
5. A. Hulsbosch: *God's Creation* (N.Y.: Sheed & Ward, 1965).
6. Thomas Merton: *Contemplation in a World of Action* (Garden City, N.Y.: Doubleday, 1971).
7. St. Basil: *Homily 12*, 4: *PG* 31; 393.
8. St. Ambrose: *Expositio in Ps. CXVIII*, 8th Sermon, 22; *PL* 15; 1503.
9. Pope Paul VI; in: *The Teachings of Pope Paul VI* (Wash. D.C., 1972).
10. *The Pope Speaks* 16 (1972).
11. *Overseas Development Council: U.S. Policy and the Third World: Agenda, 1983* (Wash. D.C.: Praeger, 1983); Table C.3.
12. George Mangatt: "Jesus and Service", in: *Jeevadhara*; no. 22, 1972 (Alleppey, India) pp. 276-277.
13. Michael H. Crosby, OFM Cap.: *Praying the Our Father as Subversive Activity* (Maryknoll, N.Y.: Orbis Books, 1977).
14. Gustavo Gutierrez: *We Drink from our own Wells*; tr. Matthew J. O'Connell (Maryknoll, N.Y.: Orbis Books, 1984).
15. Thaddee Matura: *Gospel Radicalism*; tr. Maggi Despot and Paul Lachance (Maryknoll, N.Y.: Orbis Books, 1984).
16. M.H. Crosby, OFM Cap.: *Spirituality of the Beatitudes* (Maryknoll, N.Y.: Orbis Books, 1982).
17. Max Picard: *The World of Silence*; op.cit.